As for my watch, it was what we used to call pure chicken shit. I was dressed in my whites, those silly leggings, and a pistol belt. I had a .45-caliber automatic in the belt, but I don't really know what for. I sure as hell wasn't going to shoot anybody. My job was to make sure all the men had the uniform of the day on, their hats squared away right, and weren't smoking unless the smoking lamp was lit. You know, all that nitty-gritty crap.

Well, I had no sooner got to my position, when I heard a loud explosion over on Ford Island. I looked up and I saw all these planes....

"Oh my God," I said to myself. "The Japanese are attacking us."

I ran over to a phone to call the officer of the desk, but before I got there, they sounded General Quarters.

"This is not a drill," the guy kept announcing over and over....

Berkley Books by Henry Berry

SEMPER FI, MAC

"THIS IS NO DRILL!": LIVING MEMORIES
OF THE ATTACK ON PEARL HARBOR

Most Berkley Books are available at special quantity discounts for bulk
purchases for sales promotions, premiums, fund-raising, or educational use.
Special books, or book excerpts, can also be created to fit specific needs.

For details, write: Special Markets, The Berkley Publishing Group, 375
Hudson Street, New York, New York 10014.

"THIS IS NO DRILL!"

Living

Memories

of the

Attack on

Pearl Harbor

HENRY BERRY

BERKLEY BOOKS, NEW YORK

A Berkley Book
Published by The Berkley Publishing Group
A division of Penguin Putnam Inc.
375 Hudson Street
New York, New York 10014

Copyright © 1992 by Henry Berry
Text design by Tiffany Kukec

PRINTING HISTORY
Berkley mass-market edition / December 1992
Berkley trade paperback edition / May 2001

Berkley trade paperback ISBN: 0-425-17916-8

The Penguin Putnam Inc. World Wide Web site address is
http://www.penguinputnam.com

This book has been registered with the Library of Congress.

PRINTED IN THE UNITED STATES OF AMERICA

10 9 8 7 6 5 4 3 2 1

Contents

Preface

◆

It was almost one o'clock, Sunday afternoon, December 7, 1941. I had been excused from our Sunday dinner even though my mother wasn't very happy about it.

"It's your loss, Henry," Mother said. "We're having roast beef, you know."

I felt she was probably right, but if you didn't make the first showing at the Central Theater, you had to wait in line forever for the next one. The new Amos 'n' Andy film was playing and that meant a full house.

I picked up my pal, Richie Murtaugh, and we headed up Farmington Avenue on foot. The Central Theater was about a mile away.

As we came to the intersection between South and North Quaker lanes, a blond lad named Elmer Hill came running out of his apartment house on the corner. Elmer was a year or so younger than we were. He was yelling, "War! War! War!"

"Elmer," Murtaugh said, "what in the hell are you talking about?"

"It just came over the radio. The Japs have bombed Pearl Harbor."

"Well, where in the hell is Pearl Harbor?" I asked.

Murtaugh, who always seemed to know more about things than he did, answered, "It's in the Pacific, in the Philippines."

Whatever, the war we all knew was coming had come. Most

of us on the East Coast had expected it to start with Germany, but that would come a few days later.

Well, the hell with the movie. I ran home. My family was eating dinner. Mother spoke first. "Henry, what happened to Amos 'n' Andy?"

"We're at war. The Japanese have bombed our naval base at Pearl Harbor. It is in the Philippines."

"No," said Dad, "it's in Hawaii. But if those clowns have bombed Pearl, we are at war." Then he went into the living room and turned on the radio. Every station was talking about the attack, but they seemed to be saying the same thing over and over. I noticed my mother was sobbing. I went over to her.

"What's the matter, Mom?" I asked.

"I have two sons," she said. Then she hugged me.

It was a rare American household of two or more sons that was not to be affected by the events of that Sunday half a century ago.

Introduction

◆

Margaret Mitchell's great novel *Gone with the Wind* is truly an American classic. There are many millions of Americans alive today who have either read the book or seen the film.

Yet, how many of these people understand the meaning of the title? For those readers who do not, it means that the antebellum society of the old South is a lost culture or one "gone with the wind."

Well, one may say that the pre-Pearl Harbor attack society in America is also one "gone with the wind."

However, it is not the purpose of this book to examine the changes that have occurred in America over the last half century. Let it suffice to say that these changes, both technically and socially, have been enormous.

What, then, is *"This Is No Drill!"* all about? I am an oral historian. Where could I find a better single subject to study than the American veterans of the Pearl Harbor attack?

Keeping this thought in mind, I decided to interview personally as many veterans of the Japanese attack as I possibly could.

In doing this I knew I desperately needed the help of an organization known as the Pearl Harbor Survivors Association. This assistance was graciously forthcoming. Without it I could not have finished this book.

This is such a delightful organization of more than eleven thousand members that some World War II veterans stretch the truth to try to join.

"We had this one guy," said Ken Creese, national secretary and onetime president of the Association, "who attended each chapter meeting and was always ready to help in any way he could. Hell, the guy wasn't even in the Pacific when the Japs hit us.

"He said he was in the Marine detachment of the U.S.S. *Arizona*. This was a good one to pick because most of the Marines on the *Arizona* were killed on December 7. But eventually it caught up with him. I had the unpleasant task of telling the fellow that we were on to him. Everyone liked the man. It was no fun.

"Oh, he apologized, all right. Told me he hoped none of the members would hold it against him because he had lied to get in.

"Here's another one for you. One of our group's district managers had a commanding officer who was on Maui on December 7. He recently tried to join our group. Our district manager had to tell him he could not join. I don't think it bothered our DM at all. He told me his commanding officer was a son of a bitch."

OK. If you have gathered that I think highly of the Survivors, you are correct. While I originally expected to find some Archie Bunkers in the group, I found none. While five of the men I interviewed became commissioned officers later on in the war, I only talked to two who held commissions at the time of the Japanese attack.

So, using the Survivors for my foundation, I started to travel the United States for my interviews. I did manage to visit with the desired seventy. These men had originated in thirty different states, Canada, and Washington, D.C.

The U.S. Navy provided the most interviews. After all, it was the Pacific Fleet in Pearl Harbor the Japanese wanted to sink. The secondary targets of the enemy were the various aircrafts we had at the airfields, Kaneohe, Ewa, Bellows, Wheeler, and Hickam.

In my interviewing I did find several things to be true in all branches of the service.

For instance, after the two Japanese bombing and strafing waves had left, everyone felt they would invade Oahu. The Americans were not concerned with their personal fate. What worried them was whether they had the troops and ammunition to stop the Japanese. The Americans may have underestimated the Japanese before the attack, but they most assuredly overrated them the night of December 7.

None of the men I interviewed put the blame for the disaster on the two leading officers at Pearl, General Walter C. Short and Admiral Husband E. Kimmel.

If they were to put the blame anywhere, it would be on the leaders in Washington for not keeping Short and Kimmel properly apprised of what was going on between the U.S. and Japan right up until the actual attack.

Then there was the constant bitching about the World War I equipment.

"The only reason we shot down twenty-nine planes," a survivor told me, "was that those damn planes flew so low. Hell, all those bastards were laughing at us. You could see their gold teeth." Then he chuckled. "I heard that one of our group knocked the gold out of a dead pilot's mouth."

Above all, I was getting exactly what I wanted. When I was through with my year of interviewing, I felt like I, myself, had been at Pearl.

But what about the Americans stateside? What was their reaction to the news? After all, there were millions and millions of American families that were to be drastically affected by the Japanese attack.

So, I picked out ten people whose intelligence I respected. I interviewed them.

Like my Pearl Harbor veterans, these people were from all over the United States. I wanted their reaction to the Japanese attack and how it affected them. I got it.

Well, before I go any further on my crusade to get a grassroots view of what the Japanese attack was all about, we first must return to December 25, 1940, and America's last year of peace. Everyone seemed to want to make 1941 a year to remember. And in the minds of most historians, it turned out to be a humdinger.

"THIS IS NO DRILL!"

America's Rendezvous with Destiny, Christmas 1940

◈

It was the best Christmas since the beginning of the brutal Depression. The cash registers were playing a merry tune throughout the land. It truly appeared that FDR's campaign song of "Happy Days Are Here Again" was finally coming to pass.

This was particularly true for the Berry family. My father and his brother were proprietors of a clothing store located in the center of Hartford, Connecticut. It had been in our family since shortly after the Civil War.

In a business like ours, Christmas was crucial. A bountiful holiday season could make the year. 1940 turned out to be the best year so far experienced by the venerable store.

While I was only fifteen years old at the time, I had spent my Christmas vacation working at the store. So had my older brother, Harold, and his friend, Wee Willie Walker. Mr. Walker, the epitome of sartorial splendor, stood six feet seven inches tall. Thus the nickname, Wee Willie.

My dad had closed the store at seven o'clock sharp on Christmas Eve. The Berrys and Wee Willie piled into a Yellow Cab and headed for home in West Hartford, Connecticut. As we passed St. Joseph's Cathedral on Farmington Avenue, Uncle Ed tipped his hat (everybody wore hats in those days) as was his custom. Wee Willie had been noticing this for three weeks.

A mile or two farther up Farmington Avenue we approached the Mark Twain Diner. It was at this oasis that Walker and my brother frequently consumed huge amounts of beer.

1

As we passed the Mark Twain, Willie, who was not very religious, diligently tipped his hat. I don't think Uncle Ed noticed that his leg was being pulled. My brother and I tried to stifle our laughter.

Well, that was what it was like in 1940 in our peaceful lives. The goose was hanging high. God was in his heavens and all was right with the world.

When we arrived home, we started getting ready for what would be our last peacetime Christmas for four years. It would be the last one on this planet for my beloved brother.

Opus One
City Medium

1941 had a personality of its own. It was truly a remarkable year, not really peacetime, but light-years different from the years that were to follow. Sports, entertainment, music, and all the things that are normally remembered by most people exploded. It was almost as if America was saying, "OK, we know we are going to get into this war sooner or later. But let's have a great time till it comes. And we'll start with music."

Well, you might say 1941 found a large slice of the American music world in the clutches of a onetime "phenom." No one knows when it started for sure or when it ended. Call it swing, with a touch of jazz, or just call it the Big Band Era. Call it whatever you like, but in 1941 it was "with it." It was a culture of its own and it had its own gods.

Among those at the top were the Dorsey brothers, Jimmy and Tommy. Both were destined to die young but for years their music was a national delight. The brothers started out together but went their own way in 1936.

Tommy was always the better known of the two. His nickname was "The Sentimental Gentleman of Swing." Probably his most

remembered hit started out like this: "Marie, the dawn is breaking . . ."

And if I mention Tommy Dorsey, I must include the skinny kid
from Hoboken, Frankie Sinatra. It was with Dorsey that Frank
first became a national personality. By 1991 he probably had sung
before more Americans than any other singer who ever lived.

But it was Jimmy Dorsey whose recording of "Green Eyes"
was my all-time favorite. I will always associate Helen O'Connor's
singing of "those cool and limpid green eyes" with many trips to
the Connecticut shore between Clinton and Groton in '41. I had
a teenage crush on Helen O'Connor. No doubt about that!

The other two equally popular band leaders were undoubtedly
Benny Goodman and Glenn Miller.

Goodman, by 1941 labeled the "King of Swing," led his "Let's
Dance" band through the Big Band Era. If anyone could honestly
be labeled the "Father of the Big Band Era," it should be Goodman.

In the summer of '41 Goodman signed a young singer named
Peggy Lee. She was singing with a small combo in a Chicago cocktail lounge where Goodman spotted her. Her own song, "You had
plenty money back in '22, but you let other women make a fool
of you. Why don't you do right, like some other men do?" was a
classic.

Then we come to Glenn Miller. The Miller hit songs of this
era are too numerous to list. From "In the Mood" to "Chattanooga Choo-Choo" and back again, Miller's music was the epitome of the Big Band Era.

Actually, it was Major Glenn Miller who led the campaign to
get the military bands to play the music the men wanted to hear.

Of course, there were others. If you have heard Harry James
blaring away on "You Made Me Love You," you probably
haven't forgotten it.

Well, these men and others like them dominated American music in 1941.

But it couldn't last. One could possibly say that swing was

developed for the jukeboxes of 1941. The war ended in August of
'45. Most of the World War II servicemen were civilians by De-
cember of 1946. In that one month alone, eight of the top Big
Bands broke up. They were Benny Goodman, Woody Herman,
Harry James, Tommy Dorsey, Les Brown, Jack Teagarden, Benny
Carter, and Ina Ray Hutton. The day of the Big Bands was over.

Rosebud

Of course, there was no television in 1941, but we did have
Hollywood. Most Americans who had a buck or two in their
pockets could usually be counted on to attend a film showing at
least every other week to see the Pathé News, if nothing else.

Hollywood, anxious to share in a growing prosperity, was
quite interested in satisfying the American need for entertainment.

The film industry was still taking bows for its tremendous hit
of two years before, *Gone With the Wind*. The movie was so
sensational that many filmgoers did not realize it was also one of
America's truly great novels.

Trying to capitalize on Gable's great performance as the lov-
able rake, Rhett Butler, MGM cast him in a film called *Honky
Tonk*. His costar was the young sweater-girl beauty Lana Turner.

The film was vintage Clark Gable all right. The caption at the
movie's beginning set the stage for the film. It read like this:

> *When I die,*
> *Don't bury me deep.*
> *Leave one hand free*
> *To fleece the sheep.*

The film received good reviews but not sensational ones. I enjoyed it immensely. No one realized it but the war that would
come in December was to play a very tragic role in Gable's life.
He would never be the same actor after the war as he was before

Pearl Harbor. The light of his life, his wife Carole Lombard, was killed on a war bond tour in a plane crash in 1942.

There was much more to movies in 1941 than Gable, however. MGM had found a pot of gold in the so-called middle to upper middle-class American family, the Hardys. The stately, always wise father, Judge Hardy, was magnificently played by a long-time character actor named Lewis Stone. But it was young Andy who usually stole the show. His name was Mickey Rooney and today, five decades and eight wives later, he is still captivating American audiences.

On the other side of American life, a Yankee lass who was raised across Albany Avenue from the eighth hole of the Hartford Golf Club was playing to packed houses as Tracy, the rich girl in *The Philadelphia Story*. Tracy's family in the movie was not only rich, they were filthy rich. Cary Grant and Jimmy Stewart were also in the film. Of course, the girl was Katharine Hepburn.

Also in 1941, the military had arrived in the person of two veteran burlesque comics, Bud Abbott and Lou Costello. The movie was entitled *Buck Privates*. Lou and Bud were real pros at creating comedy. There was a laugh a minute. However, pity the poor recruit-to-be who took the movie seriously. He would be in for a tremendous shock.

And we also had "The Road to" boys, one of the best-known duos in Hollywood history. It started in 1940 with *The Road to Singapore* and didn't end until 1962 with *The Road to Hong Kong*.

During that period Bob Hope and Bing Crosby, along with Dorothy Lamour, played some seven such movies. Their very clever patty-cake type humor was a sure money maker.

Their 1941 version was *The Road to Zanzibar*. Crosby ended up with Lamour and Hope ended up with the laughs. So what else is new?

But the best was yet to come. In 1941 Hollywood produced a movie that some experts say was the greatest film ever produced in America. It was named *Citizen Kane* and its director and star was Orson Welles, the young man who had scared the nation half to death a few years earlier. It is a thinly veiled attempt to produce a man amazingly similar to William Randolph Hearst. The aging Hearst was alive at the time and did everything to stop RKO from making the film. The old man failed at that, but he did succeed in his efforts to make sure *Kane* did not win the Academy Award that year. I am not a movie critic, but in my opinion the movie that won wasn't in the same class with *Citizen Kane*, but then few movies are.

"Jell-O Again"

Another form of entertainment in 1941 that was very cost efficient was the radio. You could buy a good Philco radio for peanuts and other than the cost of electricity, you could get anything from the Blue Coal Shadow to Fred Allen sponsored by Ipana for the smile of beauty and Sal Hepatica, for the smile of health.

One of the real bright spots was Jack Benny and Mary Livingston. They were on the air on Sunday nights at seven.

In 1941 Sunday was the big family day of the week. If your father was working, and in '41 most dads were, you would have a big dinner at around one o'clock in the afternoon. Dad would carve a roast or a chicken.

Then, if it was the winter, Mother would serve sandwiches from the afternoon's dinner. We would sit around a blazing fireplace and listen to Benny and his characters. My favorite was an actor named Rochester, played by a colored (a 1941 term) man named Eddie Anderson. Benny's humorous stinginess never phased Rochester.

Of course, it was all make-believe, but the radio feud between Benny and Allen was the highlight of both of their shows. Allen would also get in his digs on Benny's thrift.

"That guy Benny squeezes a penny so hard Lincoln has ingrown hairs."

Allen's forte was his "Allen's Alley." Each Wednesday Allen would take a stroll down the alley and call on each resident.

There was Senator Claghorn, a southern windbag; Titus Money, a down-easterner from Maine; Cassidy, an Irish comedian; and my favorite, the indomitable Mrs. Nussbaum. Her nephew was a genius. One week he was graduating Phi Beta Kaplan and the next week it was Come Louie.

As for the stars and the programs, I have just touched the tip of the iceberg. But to list them all would be meaningless.

However, you could start with "Mert and Marge" in the daytime and finish up with the creaking door of "Inner Sanctum."

Ernest Macho

As for the world of literature, 1941 opened up with Ernest Hemingway at the pinnacle of his career. His *For Whom the Bell Tolls* was selling like the well-known hot cakes.

In reality, Ernest didn't know what he had. He was asked about the plot as he was writing *For Whom the Bell Tolls*. He just shrugged his shoulders.

"I'm making it up as I go along," he replied.

The controversial part of the book was that the Communists backed the Loyalists while the Fascists backed the Rebels. Most Americans didn't give a hoot about either the far left or the far right.

Nevertheless, here it is fifty years later and the book is still in print.

Watch on the Rhine

Now for the theater. The mecca for both serious drama and musicals was Broadway, which was not easily accessible to the general American public on the whole. Therefore, in 1941 the popularity of live entertainment was way below that of Hollywood's movies.

But the war had come to Broadway. In 1941 the New York Drama Critics voted their Drama Circle Award to Lillian Hellman for her blockbusting play *Watch on the Rhine*.

The play showed the tremendous havoc that could be suffered by an American family with the introduction of fascism into their home. Ms. Hellman wrote many more plays in her lifetime, including *Toys in the Attic* that won the New York Drama Critics Award for 1960, but none of them had the crackling worldwide timeliness of *Watch on the Rhine*.

Baseball

So, the time has come for the number-one attraction for the American people in 1941, the world of sports where baseball was king.

Joe D., Teddy Ballgame, and Butterfingers Mickey.

Five decades ago baseball was at the top of the heap in professional team sports. Professional basketball was barely in existence. Football had its following, but the professional games were way below the college games in popularity. It wouldn't be until the age of television that pro football came into its own. I remember going to a New York Giants football game at the Polo Grounds in New York and I don't believe the stands were half-filled. But in '41 baseball had three great happenings and a few other important ones that made it one of the truly outstanding years in baseball history. It started out with Joe DiMaggio's tremendous streak. Les Brown and His Band of Renown had a recording of it. It was entitled "Joe, Joe DiMaggio, We Want You on Our Side."

Well, the Berry clan had driven to Boston in August of '41. We were having a late breakfast at the Hotel Kenmore after which we were going to leisurely stroll to Fenway Park to see the Red Sox play the New York Yankees. We were sitting near the newsstand.

All of a sudden this well-proportioned young man, decked out in a light gray pin-striped suit, white shirt, and conservative tie, showed up at the stand to buy a newspaper. It was the great Joe. He looked like a million dollars. After all, a decade or so later he was to marry America's famous sex goddess, Marilyn Monroe.

There was a very attractive young girl waiting on DiMaggio. She was unquestionably flustered. After Joe made his purchase and left, she turned to her friend and sang: "Joe, Joe DiMaggio, we want you on our side." Both girls then tittered.

As for the streak, on May 15 Joe hit a solid single to center field against the White Sox. He would have at least one base hit in each of his next fifty-five games. No one else in the history of major league baseball had come close to this feat, nor have they during the last fifty years.

While Joe was establishing his record, the New York Yankees were making a farce out of the American League pennant race. They would clinch the title by seventeen games around Labor Day.

But to pick up the interest after Joe's streak had ended, the League had Ted Williams's struggle to finish at .400 or over.

It went down to the wire. On the morning of the last game of the season, Williams was at .3995. In baseball parlance that turns into .400. Joe Cronin, Ted's manager, called Ted into his office.

"Ted," said Cronin, "you are at .400 now. Sit out this double-header. It means nothing."

"No," said Ted, "I want to play."

When the day was over, Ted was at .406. No one has come close to hitting .400 in the major leagues since.

In the meantime, while the pennant race in the American League had been a bummer, the National League's race had been a beauty. The Brooklyn Dodgers had won in a photo finish with the St. Louis Cardinals. The Dodgers, long the doormat of the League, were definitely the country's favorite in the World Series. And perhaps they could have won it if it hadn't been for an incident in the fourth game at Ebbets Field. Tommy Henrich was batting in the top of the ninth inning. There were two outs and two strikes on Henrich. Hugh Casey, the Dodger pitcher, threw what was alleged to be a spitball. Officially this is an illegal pitch but hard to detect.

Anyway, Henrich swung and missed. The game was over, or was it. A huge cheer started and then stopped just as quickly. Mickey Owen, the Dodger catcher, had missed the pitch and it had rolled to the backstop. The Yankees exploded and won the game. The next day they won the Series.

In those days you could walk across Ebbets Field after the game. We were doing just this when we spotted two ballpark security guards. One of these guards turned toward the other one.

"Dis is the loudest silence I ever hoird!" And that's the way it was.

The Brown Bomber

While professional baseball was the number-one team sport just prior to America's entrance into World War II, the most popular one-on-one sport was professional boxing. On June 18, 1941, one of the truly great championship fights of all time occurred at the Polo Grounds in New York City. It was between the heavyweight champion of the world, Joe Louis, and his challenger, Billy Conn of Pittsburgh.

Ever since Louis had won the title from James Braddock in Chicago back in '37, he had taken on all challengers.

As a matter of fact, by 1941 the sports writers had labeled Joe's opponents the "bums of the month club."

But Joe's upcoming fight with Billy Conn promised to be different. Billy was actually the light-heavyweight champion of the world. He'd put on some extra pounds for the fight, but these pounds were strictly muscle.

Billy was fast as lightning and for a twenty-three-year-old

youngster was a keen student of boxing. Most of Joe's opponents had been lumbering oxen such as Abe Simon and Tony Galento. His most recent fight (5/23/41) was with former champion Maxie Baer's kid brother, Buddy. The younger Baer was six feet six inches tall. Joe dropped him in six rounds.

Joe knew very little about Conn so he decided to visit Billy's training camp. Louis was impressed.

"Well," he said, "Billy loves to fight. And he's good. He's very quick, but remember he can run but he can't hide."

Anyway, Conn was an outstanding boxer. A fighter named Al McCoy should know. He had lost a decision to Conn. And he had been knocked out by Louis in the sixth round.

"Conn is a much better boxer than Louis," said McCoy, "and he can hit hard enough. I know. He tagged me really good a couple of times."

It was to be the classic fight between the lethal puncher and the master boxer. And so the fight started as Conn remembered.

"I fought my fight through twelve rounds," said Billy. "I had already won seven of them. I could coast in the last three and I would be heavyweight champion of the world.

"But I knew Joe was tired," continued Billy. "I went in for the kill. I ran into a hard right to the jaw, then two more quick punches to the head. By this time I was on my ass being counted out. I've been kicking myself ever since."

Conn would get a rematch five years later, but while in the service Billy had lost it. Joe knocked him out in the eighth.

It was Louis's last great fight. His purse was $625,916, which was by far the biggest purse of Joe's career. But by that time the Brown Bomber was in hock up to his ears to the IRS.

Well, this was just a short wrap-up on what America was like on the eve of its entrance into World War II.

FDR and the America First Committee

◆

While internally the U.S. was truly on a roll in 1941, Franklin Delano Roosevelt was having the battle of his life with the likes of Senator Burton Wheeler and the rest of the America First Committee.

FDR had finished 1940 with a tremendous victory over his isolationist opponents. The Republicans had nominated Wendell Willkie for the presidency. Not only did FDR win an unprecedented third term as President but Willkie turned out to be anything but a staunch isolationist. As a matter of fact, due to the deteriorating situation with Adolf Hitler, Mr. Willkie offered his services to FDR a few months after the election.

But the America First Committee, a very powerful organization, was indeed alive and well. This was a political movement dedicated to keeping the United States out of World War II. It was made up of some of America's most prestigious and powerful leaders, plus just about every Roosevelt hater in the land.

Its most charismatic leader was undoubtedly Charles Lindbergh, still the boyish hero of 1927 to many Americans. When Lucky Lindy talked, America listened.

And speak he did, not only in the United States but in Europe as well. Sometimes he made a lot of sense. When Hitler's army marched into Poland, the large majority of the American population wanted no part of the war starting up in Europe. It really wasn't till France fell and the possibility of doing business with a

Nazi-controlled Europe became a reality that most Americans looked very closely at what Lindbergh was saying.

If one studies his speeches in the context of what the Nazi government later did, you can take your pick. What was Lindbergh? Was he pro-Nazi or was he just convinced that Germany was going to win World War II and that the U.S. should turn America into an armed camp that Germany would not dare bother?

Anyway, Colonel Lindbergh had examined the German Air Force probably closer than any other non-German. After France fell he didn't think Great Britain had a chance to survive, or so he said.

However, there was more to the America First Committee than Lindbergh. This peace group was particularly strong in the Midwest. Colonel Robert McCormick's *Chicago Tribune* was against just about everything that Roosevelt was for and aid to Great Britain was no exception.

Another newspaperman who wanted America to stay home and mind her own business was William Randolph Hearst. Renowned as the man who almost single-handedly had caused the Spanish-American War, Hearst wanted no part of Mr. Hitler's war.

Actually the large majority of the America Firsters were law-abiding, sincere American people. Remember, it was only twenty or so years before that we had sent two million doughboys to France to fight the war to end all wars. Of these doughboys 125,000 died in uniform. Untold thousands came back to America to die within five years from the effects of the poisonous gas they had inhaled in France.

Many Americans felt their country was sucked into World War I. They didn't want it to happen again. And they had some powerful backers in Washington: Burton Wheeler of Montana, Gerald P. Nye of North Dakota, Bill Borah of Idaho, Ham Fish of New York, and Joe Martin of Massachusetts, to name just a few, were totally against the President.

Sometimes it was hard to separate the issues from the man. Franklin Roosevelt may have been elected to a record-setting four times to the White House, but he was also hated by millions. The world will never know how many members of the U.S. Senate and of the House were against aid to Great Britain just because Roosevelt was for it.

Unfortunately, the America First Committee could also count on the support of the nation's fringe groups. Worst of all was the Nazi Bund led by Fritz Kuhn. They claimed to be an American Nazi Party with no allegiance whatsoever to Adolf Hitler but they preached the same hate message one would hear in Berlin. Their main membership targets were first-generation Germans in the U.S. and their children. They did manage to gain some strength on Long Island and in New Jersey but not for long. America was not about to buy that Nazi garbage, even though the immensely popular *Life* magazine showed a Bund meeting at Madison Square Garden awash with American flags.

Next came Earl Browder and his highly disciplined American Communist Party. Like Kuhn's group, Browder's bunch claimed no backing outside of the U.S., but they were very strongly against any aid to Great Britain until Hitler attacked the Soviet Union in June of '41. After that event they were very much in favor of aid to both England and Russia.

Next we had that demon of the airwaves, Father Charles Coughlin. Hiding behind the aura of love, the backbone of his religion, the good father was another hate-monger.

What did he hate? Just about everything but especially anything that FDR endorsed. He published a regular tabloid named *Social Justice*, but it was Coughlin's conception of justice. If you read up on the long-dead Coughlin, it is hard to realize he was as popular as he was, but his radio audience would rival that of "Amos 'n' Andy."

The good father was not the only one of his type who commanded attention in 1941. There was a clown with the magnificent name of Gerald Lyman Kenneth Smith. In the early 1930s he had been a protégé of Governor Huey Long of Louisiana.

After the assassination of "King Fish" Long, Smith went out on his own. Like Coughlin he projected extremely well on the radio. Also like Coughlin, Smith was a man of the cloth and he was also undoubtedly a Fascist.

But with all their so-called followers, people like Smith and Coughlin may have been winners in radio polls but when push came to shove, they were nowhere. However, the highly organized and respectable America Firsters were another story.

"We must become the great arsenal of democracy." So spoke President Roosevelt. Like him or not, you must admit he was highly quotable. But to his enemies he was a witch doctor. In March of 1941 you were either an interventionist or an isolationist. The most recent newspaper poll in '41 showed that the majority of Americans, while they did not want war, most certainly believed in aiding Great Britain to the hilt.

But the America Firsters held strong. They fought the famous, or infamous, HR 1776. This was the Lend-Lease Bill. It came close to giving FDR carte blanche in his efforts to aid Britain.

Both sides pulled out all the stops. It wasn't only the ardent isolationists who were against Lend-Lease. People like Senator Robert Taft of Ohio and Arthur Vandenberg of Michigan feared the bill gave too much power to FDR.

Perhaps one who helped put the bill over was Wendell Willkie. He made a public statement that explained his position.

"Last fall," he said, "I ran as hard as I could against Roosevelt. It was to no avail. FDR was reelected. We are in a crisis. Roosevelt is my President now."

This was too much for Senator Gerald P. Nye, an ardent isolationist. It was now March of 1941. Nye reminded Willkie of his speech of October 30 of the previous year.

"You did say, Mr. Willkie, that if FDR was reelected, America could expect to be at war by April of this year. How do you feel now?"

Willkie just laughed. "Oh, that was just campaign oratory," he said.

While it can't be said that FDR and Willkie ever became good friends, Wendell was a staunch supporter of not allowing England to fall right up until his death in 1944.

Another Republican source of aid to the President came from Roosevelt's secretary of the Navy. Frank Knox spent considerable time studying the situation. Then he spoke: "Mr. President, I just can't see how Great Britain can stay in business without a tremendous amount of help from the U.S., and any way you look at it, we just can't allow the English to be defeated by Nazi Germany."

So, on March 8, 1941, the Senate passed HR 1776. Lend-Lease was now in action. But the America Firsters were not quitting. They were putting incredible pressure on everything that smacked of the military. They came within a whisker of really fouling up the entire American military buildup program.

In September of 1940 the U.S. had instituted the first peacetime draft in the country's history. As the summer of 1941 arrived, many of those already drafted were counting the days until they could go home.

But it was a complex situation. Roosevelt was empowered to extend the service of the million or so men in the Army by declaring a national emergency. However, he felt it would be better if Congress would extend the length of service by vote.

So, that is what happened on August 12, 1941, but it was frighteningly close. The final tally was 203 to 202 in favor of extending the draft.

Far from accepting reality, many of the America Firsters had bitterly fought the extension of the draft. Senator Wheeler even had thousands of postcards mailed out to soldiers asking them to complain to their congressmen about their plight.

Wheeler really went after the draftees. His theme was "Why make twenty-one dollars a month when on the outside you can make ten times as much? After all, you have put your time in!"

The most ironic part of the very close vote was that one of the very few Communists in Congress who had voted against the draft the year before had now voted for the extension. After all, Hitler had invaded the Soviet Union in June of '41. The far left in America was now calling for aid to Russia along with that to England.

Then, on September 27, came a blockbuster. Italy, Germany, and Japan had signed the Tripartite Pact. It stated that if any country not involved in the European war or the Sino-Japanese conflict attacked any of the three signees, it would be like attacking all three. In other words, it was a loaded pistol aimed at Uncle Sam's head.

In the light of the information that was uncovered after World War II, we now know the Japanese military had already developed their Pearl Harbor attack plan.

On October 30, the U.S.S. *Reuben James*, an American destroyer, was sunk off the coast of Ireland. It was helping to guard a British convoy carrying American goods to England. One hundred fifteen American sailors were lost. As the U.S. Navy had been prepared to sink any German submarines that they ran into, there really wasn't much the U.S. could do about it.

The America Firsters simply shook their heads. "What do you expect?" they said.

In reality, with a Japanese task force just about to sail for Pearl Harbor, the isolationists' cause was lost but they were to go down fighting.

Incidentally, the Congress voted on a bill to repeal completely the Neutrality Act the Monday after the *Reuben James* went down. It passed by a 50–37 vote. Better than 40 percent of the congressmen still did not feel that war was upon us.

In the meantime, while most of the press coverage was still given to Europe, the seriousness of the declining Japanese-American relationship had come to the surface.

This brings up an interesting sidelight. While the Japanese task force was headed toward Pearl Harbor, both the U.S.S. *Enterprise* and the U.S.S. *Lexington* were delivering airplanes to American bases throughout the Pacific. What if patrol planes had spotted the Japanese task force? Should they have attacked the Japanese force, or should they have returned to their respective carriers?

And the same applies to some of the many other American ships, such as the U.S.S. *Indianapolis*, a cruiser.

We know now that the captains of these American ships had been told to use their own discretion. The Japanese would have undoubtedly attempted to sink any U.S. Navy ships they ran into.

But neither the Japanese nor the Americans spotted any of the other's ships. By an extraordinary feat of seamanship, or a good deal of good luck, Admiral Nagumo succeeded in getting through to an attack position without being spotted.

All right. On December 7, 1941, the America Firsters had called for a giant meeting to be held at the Soldiers' and Sailors' Memorial Hall in Pittsburgh, Pennsylvania. The speakers were to be Senator Gerald P. Nye of North Dakota and Vernon Castle's widow, Irene. Nye, a very well known senator, loved to take Roosevelt apart at the seams. One would sometimes wonder was he sincere in his belief in isolationism or was he one of those whose hatred for FDR knew no bounds?

Well, Irene's first husband and dancing partner, Vernon, had been killed in World War I. She had a son of military age. She told the audience how much she did not want to lose her son in the current war.

When she finished talking, a United States Army colonel walked into the hall. He was in civilian clothes. He was not an isolationist. He spoke right up.

"Mr. Speaker, please, can I ask a question? I wonder if you good people realize that the Japanese have attacked our fleet at Pearl Harbor? We are now at war with Japan."

The reaction to the colonel's words was extremely hostile. Such statements as "Throw the bum out" was one of the milder phrases hurled at the colonel. He and his wife were escorted out of the hall.

It was not until the meeting was over that Senator Nye told

the audience that the report was true. The United States and Japan were at war.

Nye undoubtedly realized that when the word went out that Japan had hit the U.S. with a sucker punch, to tear into the President would be in poor taste. For instance, here is what Senator Vandenberg said on December 8: "Yesterday ended isolationism for any realist."

And so it went, right down to the wire. It was not really until the eleventh of December 1941 that the isolationists let up on FDR. It was on that day that Hitler declared war on the U.S. Within six months he took up arms against two nations, the Soviet Union and the U.S.A., that had many times the natural resources of Germany and Japan put together. The Soviet Union alone had a larger population than Germany and Japan. One could make a good case for saying that Hitler lost the war on December 11, 1941.

Why the Pacific War?

◆

For fifty years many historians have asked the same question. Namely, why was anyone amazed at what Adolf Hitler tried to do? After all, he had outlined all his plans in his book *Mein Kampf*. It was all there in black and white for the whole world to see.

Well, in 1936 the Telegraph Press of New York City published the translation of a Japanese book entitled *Japan Must Fight Britain*. Its author was a lieutenant commander in the Japanese Imperial Navy named Tota Ishimaru.

In 1936 Great Britain was assumed to have the strongest navy in the world. It was the British Navy that Japan copied the most when it decided to build the Imperial Fleet. Japan's dream of a Greater East Asia Empire could not be stopped by the British fleet, or so thought Tota.

He did point out the strong possibility of the United States jumping into such a conflict on the side of the British. He still felt the Japanese could handle both countries in a Pacific war.

Besides, he also felt that America would be inclined to stay neutral in a Japanese-British war. Japan would look to the U.S. for huge amounts of oil and military supplies.

This thought is, of course, a fantasy. But the important theme of the commander's book is that it maps out Japan's plans of conquest for Asia.

By 1936 the Japanese military was definitely gaining the upper hand in Tokyo. Their cry was "Asia for the Asians." They wanted the "round eyes" no farther in the Pacific than the Aleutian Islands. They already controlled Korea and Formosa. But that was just for openers. In 1931 their plan for conquest really exploded with an extensive invasion of Manchuria.

The Japanese force was called the Kwantung Army. For the next decade this army waged war first against the Manchurians, then against the Chinese. It grew immensely powerful and much to the chagrin of the Tokyo government almost a law unto itself.

A Japanese officer, while serving in Manchuria, would grow in stature to such an extent that his fame became known throughout the Empire. The troops called him "the Razor" due to his uncanny ability to slice through details to get things done. His name was General Hideki Tojo.

Because of the Kwantung Army's aggression in Manchuria, Japan received sanctions by the League of Nations. Their emperor was embarrassed, but the Army thought it was a joke. Yosuke Matsuoka, the Japanese delegate to the League, packed his bags and quickly returned home. This was just the first blow to the League of Nations during the 1930s. The grip of the military was tightening. There was resistance in Tokyo, but it lacked the power and the resolve to stand up to the Army.

The next move concerned an incident at the Marco Polo Bridge near Peking. It started with a firefight between Japanese and Chinese troops on July 7, 1937.

Who fired first? Who knows? But on July 26 a Japanese ultimatum was delivered to the Chinese insisting that Chinese troops withdraw from the Peking area at once. Another Chinese versus Japanese war had started. It would not end until August of 1945 when Japan surrendered.

One world leader who was infuriated by the Japanese action was FDR. In a speech in Chicago he called for a quarantine of all aggressor nations. What could be considered Japan's reply to FDR's speech occurred on December 12, 1937.

The U.S.S. *Panay*, a gunboat, had gone up the Yangtze River

toward Nanking. Its mission was to help evacuate American na-
tionals from a war zone. In order to make sure the *Panay* was
easily recognized as an American ship, it was flying an oversize
American flag.

Nevertheless, a wave of Japanese bombers descended on the
ship. It was quickly sunk. To make matters worse the Japanese
pilots then strafed the swimming American sailors. Before it was
over, four blue jackets of the American Navy were killed.

Tokyo may have been as shocked as Washington but not the
Army in the field. The Japanese Air Force colonel responsible for
the *Panay* attack admitted several years later that this was no mistaken identity. The pilots knew exactly what they were doing.

Of course there were apologies coming from all over Japan.
There was no question but that Tokyo did not want war.

Neither did the U.S. With an army the size of the Netherlands',
America was in no shape to go to war with Japan. The President
even sent a letter to the emperor telling him to put a bridle on the
runaway cannon the Japanese had in China. The letter arrived in
Tokyo, but it is doubtful it ever reached the emperor. After the
war the U.S. Army had a chance to check all the emperor's cor-
respondence. The letter was nowhere to be found.

But what happened a few weeks after the sinking of the *Panay*
was to show the world what they were dealing with when the
Japanese Army captured Nanking. Back in the Middle Ages when
an army captured a city, the victorious army was allowed to plun-
der the town.

And that is just what happened. The Rape of Nanking belonged in A.D. 900, not 1937. But it happened and over two hundred thousand civilians were massacred in a bloody orgy that
lasted over two months. By the start of 1938 the average American
was disgusted with the Japanese in general.

I was twelve years of age at the time. It seems to me that the
four dead sailors from the *Panay* were remembered more by lads
like me than the so-called adults. There were a series of cards you
could buy with bubble gum. They were called War Cards. I had

cards showing tied-up Chinese prisoners being bayoneted by Japanese soldiers.

There was another card entitled "The Rape of Nanking." But the most valuable card of all was entitled "The *Panay* Goes Down." This picture showed a half-submerged American gunboat going under with the American flag still waving above the water. That card alone was enough to sour me personally on the Japanese of fifty years ago. At that time Japan was the epitome of what happens when a country comes under the iron hand of a military dictatorship.

During this period there were many people in Tokyo who were trying to halt the march of the military toward war. But it was like trying to stop a flood.

In 1924 the United States had passed an immigration law that made it almost impossible for a Japanese to immigrate to the United States. Losing face in the Orient is a serious insult. Japan lost a lot of face when our government as much as said that their citizens were not wanted in the U.S.

There was a group in the French Air Force called the Lafayette Flying Corps in 1916. It was mainly made up of American college lads flying for the French. A glamorous lot, they received great press in the U.S. These dashing airmen played their part in the propaganda drive to turn the American mind against Imperial Germany.

Well, in 1940 a former U.S. Army pilot and stunt flyer started his famous Flying Tigers. His name was Claire Lee Chennault. He drew the same type of idealistic and adventurous young Americans to his group that had gone to France in 1916. Using revolutionary flying tactics developed by Chennault, the Flying Tigers were soon knocking down Japanese Zeros like kingpins. Japan protested to Washington, but this time it was the Japanese who ran into the blank stare. These excellent fliers remained a thorn in the Japanese side until the end of the war.

Well, as 1941 progressed so did the hostilities between Japan and the U.S. As a result of Roosevelt's battle with the America

First Committee, America's relations with Japan never got the press that the U.S. relations with Nazi Germany did.

But when it was all said and done, it got down to one word, OIL. The Japanese Imperial Fleet ran on oil. In 1941 Japan was buying most of its oil from the United States. In July of 1941 Washington froze all Japanese assets in the U.S. This would eventually make it impossible for Japan to continue its all-out war of aggression in China and the rest of Asia.

But the Japanese had anticipated this act. Admiral Nagumo had designed a fast-moving plan to use the whole Imperial Fleet to capture the East Indies oil-producing islands before the U.S. Pacific Fleet could get out of Pearl Harbor.

By the time the U.S. fleet had arrived near Japan, the Japanese fleet, with its ten aircraft carriers, could destroy the U.S. fleet in Japan's home waters. This had been mapped out in the late 1930s. But the most prestigious man in the Japanese Navy, Isoroku Yamamoto, had other plans. He had visions of the bulk of the Japanese fleet being in the East Indies and the U.S. fleet coming over and finishing off what was left around Japan.

Anyway, Yamamoto had spent many years in the United States. He had even taken a two-year course at Harvard University.

Above all, he studied the American people. He knew not only of the mighty industrial power of the United States but also the pride Americans took in their country. It wasn't an intensely paternalistic pride such as the Germans and the Japanese had; it was a much lower-key pride. But it was there and the Americans would fight for it.

So, Yamamoto came up with a different plan. The Japanese would load up six of their ten aircraft carriers. They would come at Pearl Harbor from the north on a Sunday morning in December. The damage done to Pearl Harbor would be immense.

Yamamoto knew a surprise strike at Pearl was so revolutionary that the Americans wouldn't even consider it. And with a few exceptions he was right.

It was the same with the Japanese admirals. Would they or

would they not fight the United States? This was definite; if the U.S. shut off their oil, they would have no choice but to fight.

There was one man in the government who at least questioned the wisdom of going to war with the U.S. His name was Shigenori Togo, the foreign minister. After being told that as negotiations had broken down, the only choice was war, he commented: "Just because we can no longer negotiate with the Americans, must we bomb them?" For that remark alone he should have been given a medal.

So be it. On October 17, 1941, General Hideki Tojo, Japan's war minister, replaced Prince Konoye as prime minister. He retained his position as War Minister. Now, both the civilian government and the military were under one man.

Tojo was a career military man in the best samurai tradition. However, he was dedicated to the Japanese plans for expansion in Asia. While men like Tojo and Yamamoto were completely honest men, they, like most Japanese leaders, firmly believed that the Japanese people were the chosen people of the East, if not the world. They were born to lead, or so these men thought.

So, while many historians think that the appointment of Tojo played a big part in starting the war, plans for the Pearl Harbor attack were made long before he got the big job.

So, with all the meetings and hoopla, the question of peace or war came down to one controversy. It was like teenagers playing chicken.

Japan said, "You must sell us oil." America replied, "We will sell you oil as long as you start withdrawing your troops from French Indochina."

The whole thing brings up a moral question. Did the United States have the right to tell Japan what she must do?

On the other hand, did Japan have the right to tell the U.S. to whom it must sell its oil? Take your pick.

An interesting aside. Would Japan have taken on the U.S., Great Britain, and the Netherlands if the Netherlands had not been conquered by Germany and if England wasn't fighting Germany for its life?

Whatever, Japan did bomb the island of Oahu on December 8 (Japanese time), 1941, forcing the U.S. into World War II. Now, it's Don Seaton's turn to tell us his reaction to the Japanese attack.

Don Seaton—U.S.S. *Indianapolis*

I wasn't at Pearl very long before the *Indianapolis* received sailing orders. On December 5, 1941, we were to go out on patrol to a godforsaken place called Johnson Island.[1] We knew the peace talks in Washington (D.C.) had bogged down and that the outlook was quite bleak. But none of us really had a clue on what was about to happen.

So, we were ready to shove off when this lieutenant junior grade called us together.

"Men," he said, "stand to. It's quite likely that this patrol will be the real thing. You all know that a two-man Nip submarine washed up on Maui the other day, and several other Jap subs have been spotted all over the area. It is quite possible that a shooting war will break out any day. Be ready for it."

Well, I stayed on the *Indianapolis* for the next two years and we were never again on the full alert we were on as we steamed out of Pearl.

At the time I was a gunner on one of the cruiser's airplanes. We were on the catapult ready to take off on a minute's notice.

---

[1] Johnson Island is one of the most isolated places in the Pacific. Everyone talked to the large colony of gooney birds that lived there. But when the birds started talking back, the powers that be figured the lad had had enough. They sent him stateside.

We had depth charges under our wings. The pilot was a guy named Joe Mulhauser.

It was like this throughout the ship. Every man was at his battle station. Those guys weren't going to take us by surprise.

And remember, as far as we knew, we weren't at war with anyone. At no time over the next two years were we that ready for an attack. We just didn't have the manpower.

Anyway, we were still on full alert two days later when we got the word about the Japanese attack.

Wow, we just couldn't believe it. How in the hell did they get to Pearl without being seen? And what kind of a reception did they get? We had been told that Pearl was the Gibraltar of the Pacific.

Remember, this was 1941. Americans didn't think very highly of the Japanese. We figured our boys had knocked the hell out of the attackers. What a shock was in store for us when we returned to Honolulu.

We finished our patrol without spotting any Japanese, which really pissed us off. I didn't know what one cruiser could have done to the Imperial Japanese fleet, but we were sure eager to try. So, we headed back to port.

As we approached Pearl, I was fore with a pair of binoculars and was waiting for my first glimpse of the harbor. When I got it, I couldn't see anything wrong, but as we got closer and closer I figured something was screwy.

A shipmate of mine also had binoculars. All of a sudden he let out a yell.

"Christ," he bellowed, "those silhouettes are cockeyed."

Then I noticed several of the battleships were partially underwater. The closer we got, the more we could see the utter disaster that had struck Pearl.

I can remember this World War I CPO with tears in his eyes, shaking his head.

"Take a good look, you clowns. You're seeing the end of the old battlewagon Navy that I loved so much. From here on in, it will be the carriers that are important. Thank God, none of ours were at Pearl on the seventh. Uncle Sam will be building so fuckin' many flattops, those bastards will have 'em coming out of their assholes."

The old-timer was right. And it wasn't only the ships that would change. I don't think that more than fifteen percent of the sailors in the fleet were USNR when the war started.

It was still the old Navy of those *Saturday Evening Post* stories; where someone named Pug Larson was the heavyweight champion of the fleet. Do you remember the movie when Dick Powell sang "Shipmates Stand Together"? To the civilians, the U.S. Navy was all fun and games. My God, how that was going to change!

Another change was going to occur. This was how we looked at the Japanese, or Japs and Nips as we called them. And that was when we felt charitable.

Most of the time we called them a lot worse. After all, it was a sneak attack. In America we called it a sucker shot. And if you were on the square, you didn't go around taking sucker punches at people.

Besides, we all had shipmates at Pearl when the Japanese struck. There was a sailor, who had been at radio school with me back in Chicago in the fall of '40. As I remember it, he was killed on the *Pennsylvania*. The *Pennsy* had been in dry dock when the bombers came in. The poor guy. He probably never knew what hit him.

Another buddy of mine was named Mills. I can't remember his first name, but he was in boot camp with me in San Diego. One day I can remember real well was when the two of us had gone to sick bay to get out of some detail.

You see, there was a movie on the base we both wanted to see. I can't remember what it was, but it probably featured Clark Gable; old big ears was a favorite of mine.

So, we figured if we went to sick call and told the corpsman we had cat fever, they'd give us some pills and send us on our way.

Wouldn't you know it? We both had a temperature of about one hundred. There was a flu epidemic floating around, so we both spent the next four days in sick bay. Missed the movie altogether.

So, as we pulled into Pearl, I noticed this tall, lanky guy steering a launch all around the oily harbor. My God, it was Mills. I knew he'd been on the *West Virginia*, but what I didn't know was he'd been a hell of a hero during the attack, picking up wounded men who were trying to swim through that oil. His launch had saved many a sailor. And all this was done under fire.

A few days later, I looked him up. We drank some beer and he told me all about the attack. I never saw Mills again. Hope he made it through the war.

Anyway, one thing was a certainty. It was going to be a long war. Any navy that could travel as far as the Japanese had and then deliver the knockout blow they did, sure as hell wasn't going to be a pushover.

Well, what now was the Navy to do with these sailors whose ships had either been sunk or put out of action for repairs? Couldn't let them sit on their ass with a war going on.

So, they started to disperse them throughout the fleet. One of the men who came to the *Indianapolis* was Dorey (Doris) Miller. Dorey was a very powerful black man who had been the heavyweight champion of the *West Virginia*, and what a hero he had been on December 7.

It seems that when Captain Mervyn Bennion of the *West Virginia* was mortally wounded in the stomach with shrapnel, his communications officer, Commander Beattie, sent for Miller.

"Get that big messman, Dorey Miller. He's strong enough to carry the captain to sick bay."

And so he was, but the captain died shortly after they got him below.

After he left sick bay, Miller noticed an unattended .50-caliber machine gun. Its firer had been shot out of its harness. Even though Miller had never fired a machine gun, he stepped right into position and kept the gun blazing until the attack was over. I believe Miller was the first black man to be awarded the Navy Cross.

When Miller came aboard, my curiosity was piqued. I had never met a holder of the Navy Cross before, black or white. I went out of my way to get to know him. He wasn't a militant black; they would come later. But he sure as hell was no step'n'fetchit colored man either. He didn't have much education, but you could tell he was sharp as a whip just by talking with him.

Take that machine-gun episode. Miller was not only smart but brave as hell. I used to look at Miller and shake my head.

"What the hell is an outstanding man like that doing as a mess-man?" I'd say to myself.

There were changes coming aplenty, but they would be too late for Miller. I left the *Indianapolis* in the early part of '43. Miller had already gone back to the States by then, I heard that he had eventually gone back to the Pacific and was killed by a kamikaze plane off Okinawa. Too bad. Miller would have gone a long way in today's Navy.

Be that as it may, I served right through to the end of the war and saw plenty of action. But the two things I remember the most vividly are the incredible state of readiness the *Indianapolis* was in when we sailed out of Pearl on December 5, and the scene of utter destruction that greeted us when we returned three weeks later. How could the fleet have been caught with its pants down, so to speak, just two days after we left?

Bully for Claude Swanson

◆

Five days short of four years before the Japanese attacked Pearl Harbor, an American gunboat was on the Yangtze River near Nanking. It was trying to evacuate U.S. citizens from what was definitely a war zone. It was flying a very large American flag. It had every right to be doing what it was doing.

Then, out of nowhere, appeared several Japanese bombers. They quickly sank the *Panay*. To add insult to injury, they strafed the American sailors, killing four of them.

Washington, D.C., was aghast. Roosevelt was outraged. It was true that the Pacific area was always a sideshow to FDR—the big arena was Europe—but this Japanese treachery could not be ignored. It called for action. The President called an emergency meeting of his Cabinet. He called on his secretary of the Navy, Claude Swanson. There was dead silence for a moment. Then the aging and quite infirm Mr. Swanson slowly rose.

"Mr. President, I have been accused of being a pacifist and perhaps rightly so." At this point his voice was barely above a whisper. He cleared his throat in an attempt to gather strength. "But a dastardly act such as the Japanese murdering our boys can only be answered with . . ." He stopped once again to build up his strength. Now he shouted, "can only be answered with war."

Then the old man slumped back in his seat. Mr. Swanson was not to be in the Cabinet much longer, nor had he long to live. But for a few minutes in 1937 he was beautiful. As people were wont to say a half century ago, "The old man knew his onions."

Why Did No One Believe It?

At a meeting of the Pearl Harbor Survivors in Oceanside, California, I tried to get an answer to why no one believed the Japanese would come all the way to Pearl Harbor to start their war and why so many things were totally snafu on December 7, 1941.

I pointed out that there are so many questions still unanswered and as each year goes by, the chances they will ever be answered diminish greatly.

One of the survivors I talked to told me that the first warning he knew of had come from Ambassador Joseph Grew in Tokyo. And that warning had occurred in early 1941.

Another survivor talked about the two Army privates in charge of the radar facility at the Opana station on the northern tip of Oahu. Their names were George Elliott and Joe Lockard.

One can just imagine these two, bored out of their heads while waiting for the breakfast wagon and probably more or less just playing with the radar machine. Wham, they hit the jackpot!

To use a World War II expression, I'll bet dollars to doughnuts one of the two uttered an amazed "Holy shit!"

Of course they did try to report to headquarters that they had more planes on the radar screen than they'd ever seen before but to no avail. They were told not to worry about it.

Then our group discussed the telephone warning that had come from the sailor at the Kaneohe Naval Air Station across the island from Pearl. A naval officer had told the caller to sober up. I wonder how that officer felt ten minutes later when the first Japanese planes showed up over Pearl Harbor?

Next, we have the radio operator on the U.S.S. *Ward*. The *Ward* actually sank a Japanese submarine right outside the entrance to Pearl Harbor at least an hour before the attack. Admiral Kimmel was not told of this till after the attack started. He was livid. It seems a junior officer did not think it was important enough to bother the brass with.

On and on our conversation dragged. Everybody seems to have known that the Japanese were going to hit the U.S. with tremendous force but the logical place seemed to be the Philippines.

Finally, a onetime sailor on the *West Virginia* spoke up. He was obviously a believer in predestination.

"The attack was bound to be. There was nothing anyone could have done about it. It was our destiny."

That was enough for our group. I don't know how many people really believed him, but that was it.

Sergeant John Caputo, 24th Squadron—U.S. Army Air Corps

RICK: If it's December 6 in Casablanca, what time is it in New York City?

SAM: I don't know, boss.

RICK: I'll bet they're asleep in New York City. I'll bet they're asleep all over America.

> —a conversation between a heavy-drinking Rick and his piano player, Sam, in the film *Casablanca*

So, Ed Gunger told you about the ladies of Hotel Street showing up at our hospital shortly after the attack was over. And he wanted me to confirm it, did he?

Hell, yes, I'll confirm it. The dust had hardly settled when we saw this bus pull up in front of our hospital and all these young ladies stepped out. This guy who was standing next to me started to wave his arms.

"Hey, Molly," he yelled out, "do you remember me?"

And Molly yelled back, "We figured we'd be needed to help out here. We're Americans too, you know."

Then I spotted this fat middle-aged woman in a red dress. The young soldier next to me seemed to know her also.

"Hell, Joe," he said, "there's Big Momma; she runs the best cathouse in town with an iron hand."

Well, Big Momma is giving the girls the word.

"All right, ladies, now behave yourselves. These are our boys those Jap bastards have bombed. And we're here to help any way we can. Anything they want us to do, we are going to do. Remember, no hanky-panky."

Oh, these girls were there a whole day ahead of the Red Cross workers. They were the salt of the earth.

You see, a great many of them were college students from the San Francisco Bay area. They would fly over to Pearl Harbor, spend a few months on Hotel Street, make a bundle, then fly back to the mainland. They were just working their way through college on their backs, that's all.

Besides, when the Red Cross girls took over the hospital work, the ladies of the evening went to work to help us get food. Our mess hall had been bombed to hell. Feeding us had become a real problem.

All right. I was born in Franklin, Massachusetts. When my mother died, Dad moved the family to the Hartford area. In 1934 I graduated from Hartford Public High School, one of the oldest high schools in the country. Work was hard to find, but I finally got a job with an electrical supply firm.

Then I had a brainstorm. Join the Navy and see the world. I went over to the recruiting office in New Britain. The physical and written tests were a snap. I thought I was in, but it was no soap.

"Sorry, young man," I was told. "Your bite is off center with a couple of your teeth. You're out of luck."

So, the hell with them. I was really pissed off.

"Oh," I said, "if we have a war, am I supposed to bite the enemy?"

Anyway, I went back to Hartford and tried the Army Air Corps. I'd always been very interested in flying. However, my reception was cold.

"There's no room for you, son. We're full up for a year or two. With this depression Uncle Sam is cutting down on everything. Come back in two years."

You see, whenever times are bad, kids in their teens flock to the recruiting office. The sergeants were in seventh heaven. They could pick and choose. I knew a lot of kids my age who ended up in the three C's because for one reason or another they weren't up to mustard for the military.

Well, about two years later I went into this diner on Asylum Avenue, over near the railroad station. Who's there but the Air Corps recruiter.

"Hey, Caputo," he says, "do you remember me? The Army Air Corps has some openings now. Do you want in?"

"Do I ever," I answered, "hell, I'm not going back to work even to pick up my paycheck!"

"Caputo, that's the spirit we like. We'll process you in a hurry."

Boy, did they work fast! I was a private in the Air Corps before you could say Jack Robinson. There was another guy, name of Love, who enlisted with me. They told us we could go to any Air Corps field in the U.S., Hawaii, Panama, or the Philippines.

So, Hawaii sounded great to me. Whenever you'd see a movie about Honolulu, these gorgeous girls were swinging their tushes and singing about beautiful Hawaii.

Love agreed. We both picked Luke Field on Ford Island at Pearl Harbor and we never regretted it.

Think back for a second. What if we had picked Clarke Field in Luzon? If we weren't killed by the Japanese attack there, we would have both spent the war in a Japanese prison camp. The hell with that!

As it was, I found the Hawaiian Islands to be great. Oh, some of the big hotels didn't exactly welcome servicemen unless they had bars on their shoulders, but the hell with 'em. The rest of the places had the welcome mat out for you, if you had a buck in your pocket, that is.

And there were always organizations like the YMCA that were constantly trying to keep the servicemen from going to pot. Kind of an early-day USO.

Here's an example of what I mean. In 1939 the islands received a lot of war refugees from China. These people were White Russians from the Shantung Peninsula. The Japanese were raising hell with them.

Among these refugees were many young people. Naturally they were like fish out of water in Honolulu. The Y decided to set up a dance for the young Russian girls. I believe it was on the Fourth of July.

We had moved to the new Hickam Field by this time. A big group of us decided to go to the dance. Right after I came in, I spotted this young girl with a flower in her hair, a bit on the plump side, but not bad at all. I put on my best manners and went over and asked her to dance. I'll never forget what she said.

"Yes, but don't dance me fancy, dance me plain. I don't dance very many, but I do the best that I are."

Wow! Was she ever something!

Then a wiseass from our group started setting off firecrackers. Remember, these refugees were gun-shy anyway.

Shit, my Russian partner let out a yell, pushes me on my rear end, and took off, yelling in Russian a mile a minute. Boy, did that clear out the dance hall!

Well, as I've told you, before Uncle Sam built Hickam Field, our squadron was over on Ford Island at Luke Field. It was named after Frank Luke, a World War I pilot who specialized in shooting down German balloons.

The only drawback with Luke was getting back to Ford Island on the weekends. The last boat left at midnight.

So, a little bit of Yankee ingenuity was in order. We'd stash rowboats on the shore. This way we could get back at any hour.

Besides, the girls loved to take a moonlight ride in the harbor.

OK, have you ever seen one of those big buoys the battleships have? You'd have a few drinks and so would your girlfriend. We did all kinds of crazy things on those buoys, I mean real crazy. Of course, you didn't want to get caught. Your ass would be in a sling if they nailed you.

You see, I had been at Pearl Harbor five years when the attack came. This was the peacetime Air Corps and by and large it was a good life. To top it off, Hawaii was good duty and Squadron 24 was a great outfit.

OK, December 6, 1941, I had a '32 Chevy. A group of us had gone to a place called Kau Kau Corners. All the waitresses wore tight shorts and low bras. You could kid with 'em and they loved it. None of us had too much booze that night, but we were surely raising hell with the girls.

Then, at midnight the Honolulu radio station went off the air. We started picking up a lot of static and some Japanese voices. We paid no attention to it. In the meantime I'm getting tired. I gave the boys the word.

"Listen, we have a dozen or so new B-17s coming in later this morning. Let's go back to the barracks, get a good night's sleep, and watch our planes come in."

Everyone seemed to agree, so we took off. We got back to our quarters and kept bullshitting until we dozed off. Sunday was a relaxing day in the Army then. None of us had the foggiest idea what was going to happen the next day.

The following morning dawned and you could easily see it was going to be one of those beautiful mornings. Sometime between 0730 and 0800 we were sitting around in our skivvie drawers, discussing our breakfast. Should we go to the mess hall, the PX, or downtown?

Out of the blue we heard some planes coming in. One of our guys looked out the window.

"Hey," he said, "those are not B-17s, those are navy planes."

We all started to look out the window. Whenever Navy planes would come in from our carriers, they'd buzz the hell out of Hickam. It was a show worth seeing.

Then another guy piped up: "Yes, they're navy planes all right, but they're in the wrong blasted navy. Those are meatballs!"

Just like that, we were at war and the bastards didn't waste any time. They started in on our planes right away. They weren't going to have any of our bombers going after their fleet.

Next came some strafers. They came in real low and shot right through the barracks windows. They knocked the venetian blinds to pieces. Most of us were not really scared until they hit one of our guys in the chest with two slugs. He died quickly.

That was enough! An immense calm came over me. All I wanted was a chance to get a crack at those bastards.

We all went outside, which was smart because both the barracks and the mess hall took direct hits. I looked up and saw this big bomb coming down. I mean, you could actually see it falling.

Wham! It picked up those steel doors on the hangar, where we had our guns stored, and threw them out on the parade field.

Talk about confusion—a few months later I would realize that all battles are dominated by confusion. But this was more than confusion. It was terror in spades! Remember, one minute we are wondering where we're going to get our ham and eggs. The next minute we're being bombed to pieces.

And there are things as you look back that are now funny as hell.

For instance, there was one of those tractors we used to help ferry the planes out in the middle of the field. Two of our older sergeants were out there trying to hide behind the tractor. You could easily see that they'd spent many years sampling that starchy Army food. They both had their faces buried in their hands on the ground with their fat butts sticking up in the air.

All of a sudden an airman runs out, jumps into the seat of the tractor, and drives it off. Our two hearties are all alone in the same position.

"Get your asses down, you idiots, or they'll be blown off!" someone yelled.

The two huskies got up with sheepish grins and took off.

Another guy, a good friend of mine, had gone into one of our B-18s and had started firing a .50 caliber machine gun at the Japanese. They strafed the hell out of the plane, wounding my friend badly. They had also set the plane afire. The gunner was trapped inside and the flames were closing in all around.

"Shoot me, shoot me," he was screaming. I can hear him today. I don't think anyone shot him, but when they got him out after the raid, he was burned to a crisp. Our people were being wounded left and right.

We had a full-blooded Cherokee Indian in the 24th named Elmer Big Thunder. Elmer was a great guy until he got into the firewater, then watch out.

I can remember one time when he came back to the barracks all tanked up. He covered his face with toothpaste for war paint. He got a machete out of his survival kit. Then he chased the first sergeant out to the front gate, war-whooping all the way. They stuck his ass in the stockade for that one.

So, after the second wave was finished with us, we started to count heads. At first we couldn't find Big Thunder. Then we spotted him over by the flagpole. He was holding his stomach together with his hands. Shrapnel had ripped him open. We got him to the hospital and I'm happy to say he recovered.

All of the 24th weren't so lucky. I had a great pal named Bill Northrup. He'd been in the hospital with something or other and was just getting out. He heard all this noise and came running out to see what was going on. A bomb landed near him and some shrapnel went into his heart. He was gone. I think he was the first man from the state of Rhode Island to be killed in the war.

All right, that's what it was like. But don't confuse the Pearl Harbor Army with the lads who came later. We were still the old campaign hat Air Corps. Many of us had enlisted in the thirties, but we had plenty of old-timers from the twenties and even a few from what we used to call the Great War. One of these men was a man named Frank. He'd been a gunner in one of those old DHs that had arrived in France in the fall of 1918. Frank was even flying when he wasn't flying, if you know what I mean.

You see, Frank had made the rounds the night of December 6. He had gotten up for colors; he always did, but he was still coasting. During the attack he was calmly walking around talking to the troops. He had a bottle of beer in his hand.

"Stay cool, men," he was saying. "No use ducking. They have numerous rounds, you know."

He gave us a laugh when we needed it, but I never knew if Frank realized that his beloved Army Air Corps was disappearing with those bombs. Anyway, it wasn't too many months after the attack when I realized that Frank's days as a gunner were over.

Frank was the top turret man on one of our B-17s. You could always tell if Frank was seated because if he was, the guns would be pointed straight out.

So, later in '42 we did get into combat. Frank's plane was next to mine. All of a sudden I noticed that Frank's guns were up in the air.

"Oh, my God," I said to myself, "they've shot Frank out of his chair!"

I was wrong. Five minutes later his guns were sticking out straight. Frank was back in the fight.

Several days later I ran into Frank somewhere in the Pacific. I told him how glad I was to see him, that I'd thought he'd been shot. He just laughed.

"Hell, no," he answered, "I just stopped to have a little drinkee or two."

The next thing I heard about Frank, he'd been sent back to the States. Things had gotten a little too serious for Frank.

Another way you could tell how serious things had become was the case of our dog. He was named after a local beer called Primo. We called him that because he loved to drink beer. The boys who had the twelve to four duty in the morning used to give him all the beer he wanted. Primo would get loaded about every night and go crazy. After the attack no one seemed to have the time to give the dog any beer. I guess poor old Primo had to turn into a teetotaler.

Another thing about the attack. It was a disaster, all right. But remember, one way or another, the Americans did knock down twenty-nine Japanese planes.

All right, that wasn't many compared to the havoc the Japanese caused, but they sure could have used those twenty-nine experienced pilots they lost later on during the war. And if we had been able to get airborne all the planes we had in the Pearl Harbor area, we could have shot down a hell of a lot more of them than we did.

Anyway, many of our planes were destroyed on the ground. The Japanese dealt us a real haymaker. But it wasn't really the knockout punch they hoped for. We had everything that could fly up in the air about ten hours after the attack.

I, myself, was in a B-17 bomber that headed south. That is where we were told the attack had come from.

We knew it would be curtains for us if we spotted the Japanese fleet, but the way most of us felt we would have gladly gone down if we could have dropped some eggs on their carriers.

So, what do you know, we later found out the attack had come from the north. It seems all the dope we were getting that day was screwed up.

We got back to Pearl safely and joined all the confusion connected with the anticipated Japanese invasion. When it soon became apparent that the enemy had no thought of landing at Pearl, the powers that be began to lay plans for action.

The first thought concerned Wake Island. Half of a Marine Defense Battalion was putting up a tremendous resistance against a Japanese takeover. A relief force, including the U.S.S. *Saratoga* and the U.S.S. *Astoria*, was quickly assembled and set sail. I don't know how far they got, but it was eventually called back, much to the disappointment of the personnel aboard the ships, I may add.

Wake fell just before Christmas. The island may have been abandoned, but it was not forgotten. I was the flight engineer on a B-17D that took off for Midway Island the end of December. It was a real light plane, having no turrets.

We arrived at Midway and were given all the fuel we could possibly carry. We were then to fly to Wake, take as many photos showing what the Japanese had done to the island, and return to Midway as quickly as possible. We had a force of some four planes. We knew there would be a lot of flak thrown at us, but with the type of camera we had we could stay out of range of their guns.

So, we left Midway, flying into the teeth of the Japanese dragon. Deep down I didn't think we'd make it back to Midway. Never mind the enemy. I just didn't think we had enough gas for the trip. We had been given a spot in the ocean where we could ditch if the gas ran out. However, our orders were explicit: "Whatever happens, don't lose the camera!"

We arrived over Wake just as dawn broke. We took as many pictures as we could in a big hurry, turned around, and headed for Midway.

Now the Good Lord took a part. We got as strong a head wind on the way back as I have ever seen. I don't think we would have made it without that head wind.

But when we got to the point in the ocean where we were to ditch, the captain gave us the word.

"We're about five hundred miles from Midway," he said. "I think I can take a gradual descent and make that island."

And that's exactly what happened. Once at Midway it was a breeze getting back to Pearl. They gave us all the Distinguished Flying Cross. I think we were the first ones to get that award in World War II, other than men who had been killed.

The Tuxedo Pants Pilots

There were two young fighter pilots serving in the 47th Pursuit Squadron at Wheeler Field in the late fall of 1941. For the past two weeks or so they had been quartered at Haleiwa on the north shore of Oahu.

On the night of December 6 they had been doing what any other single, good-looking, young men would be doing. They had been making the rounds. They had ended up at the officers' club at Hickam Field. Here they had lived up to their reputations as two of the best poker players in the U.S. Army Air Corps.

Sometime in the wee hours of the morning, Ken Taylor and George Welch, the two pilots, decided their beds at Wheeler were more comfortable than the ones at Haleiwa. So, they hit the sack then and there.

Ken Taylor was awakened by the sound of the Japanese bombing. He quickly put on the first trousers he could find, which happened to be his tuxedo pants, part of his attire of the previous evening, and ran outside.

Here he ran into his buddy, George Welch. They both immediately realized what was going on.

"George," Ken said, "get a car or a truck, get something. I'll call Haleiwa and tell them to get two P-40s ready for takeoff. We're going up."

The trip to Haleiwa took about ten minutes. It was quite hairy because the Japanese were strafing every automobile they saw, but they made it and were soon airborne.

They found the Japanese at Ewa Field. There they were making mincemeat of the grounded Marine Corps Wildcats. George and Ken tore into the Japanese.

These two were probably the first American fliers the Japanese had encountered. It must have been a shock.

Anyway, the dogfights continued until the Americans ran out of ammunition. They headed back to Haleiwa for more bullets. The two Americans were quickly rearmed and were soon airborne once again. It wasn't very long before they found themselves facing the enemy.

So, once again the battle was joined, but this time the Japanese put a slug through Taylor's left arm that ended up in his leg. Legend has it that he was more concerned about his devastated tuxedo pants than his wound.

Anyway, both Taylor and Welch kept airborne until the Japanese planes headed back for their carriers. They, in effect, chased them away.

Once the Americans landed, Taylor insisted we send bombers after the carriers.

"I know where they have to be. Their planes were all headed north!"

He was politely informed that there were no bombers available. Then a doctor spoke up.

"But you better let me patch up your arm and leg."

Taylor resisted.

"Hell, no, they'll be back soon. I want another crack at 'em!"

He was overruled. Taylor and Welch were through. They were officially credited with seven kills. I know of no other American fliers who were credited with anywhere near that many kills on December 7.

But what if we could have put one or two hundred P-40s into the air that day? And if the pilots could have been as good as Taylor and Welch?

Hell, the Japanese would have been in deep trouble.

Jackson Spears—A Gentleman
Personified

◆

The regal Mr. Spears is in his mid-eighties. He is rarely seen without a coat and tie. He is a daily picture of sartorial splendor. With a voice of unusual magnitude he can hold forth on any given subject. He was born and bred in Texas—he can still tell you the date of San Jacinto Day—but has spent most of his adult life in Fairfield County, Connecticut. On a day in the spring of 1991 he was delighted to share his memories of December 7, 1941 with me. Enter Jackson.

Of course I remember Pearl Harbor. I knew we were close to war with Japan, but I never felt they'd go all the way to Pearl Harbor to attack us, but they did.

Well, we had just finished our Sunday dinner at my father-in-law's apartment in New York City. He was quite a fellow. He would frequently call his wife on a Saturday and tell her there'd be twelve to dine at noon on Sunday and that's just what he'd done. We'd finished our meal and had gone into the living room of my in-laws' apartment on Park Avenue. I leaned over and turned on the radio.

Among my in-laws' guests on that day was a half-Scottish and half-Japanese young chap. After the radio had announced the news of the Japanese attack, we all sat there stunned. When I got over that first shock, I looked at our half-Japanese friend. As I recall he wore a confused smile.

His name was George Bender. He had been working for my

father-in-law for years. It seemed to me he was both disgusted with what the Japanese had done and impressed that they had pulled it off.

Now here's another one for you. It occurred at the Woodway Country Club in Darien, Connecticut. A member over there was a very successful Japanese businessman named Arai. He was there with his son.

The Arai family had been in this country for many years. Their son may have been born here. When the radio blared out the news, the son spoke up.

"Dad," he said, "I'm going to join the American Army. What Japan has done is dreadful."

"Son," the old man said, "please wait awhile. You may not be wanted." The father was right.

Another thing that concerned me was the then Major Truman Landon. He later became one of the youngest generals in the Army Air Corps. His sister and my wife were very close friends. Well, I knew the major was headed for Pearl Harbor in command of a dozen or so B-17s. Due to our relations with Japan he had wanted to put a supply of bombs aboard and some machine-gun ammunition. Truman even called the White House and wanted to know why he had machine guns but no ammunition. He wanted to be able to defend himself if attacked.

"Absolutely not," he was told. "The last thing we want right now is an incident."

Anyway, all his planes came down right at the time of the attack. Some of them landed on a golf course. They were landing all over Oahu.

The general later told me that his planes did have some fuel left. They could have tried to find those Japanese carriers so they could drop some big bombs on them. He knew many of his planes would have been lost, maybe all of them, but he felt they could have done a job on the Japanese task force.

PFC Forrest Smith,
3rd Defense Battalion, USMC

The first enlisted Marine was recruited on the morning of November 10, 1775. The second Marine was sworn in that afternoon. He turned to the first Marine.

"Hey, mate," he asked, "is there always this much chicken shit in this lash-up?"

"Oh, hell," the first Marine answered, "you think this is bad, you should have been in the old Corps." Or so the story goes.

I guess you would definitely call me old Corps in 1991. But back in '39 if you were old Corps, it meant you has served in the "Banana Wars" and at the China station and if you were real old Corps, you had to have been in France in 1918.

You know though, my memory is so good on World War II that it is hard for me to compare myself to those old-timers from the 1930s.

But I guess you have to call me old Corps. As far as WWII is concerned anyway. Eyah, old Corps, ain't no doubt about it.

After all, I was there when it started at beautiful Pearl. And I was with the relief column that came within a hundred miles or two of Wake Island, then turned back. Think I was on the U.S.S. *Raleigh*, right near the U.S.S. *Saratoga*. And I was also on Midway Island when we stopped those Japanese cold in June of '42.

To top it off, I was on the *Okie* in '45, the last big battle of the Pacific war. As those old Union Army veterans used to say, "I seen the elephant aplenty."

Well, back to '39. I was raised in the state of Maine and I'm still here. Winterport, right near Seaport. I'm sure you know where that is. There wasn't much going on here in those days.

Haw, haw, that's a hot one. Ain't much going on here today neither.

Anyway, I'd gone to the big fair up the road around Bangor. I saw these two Marines in their dress blues at the fair. Good God Almighty, they surely looked snappy. So, I said to myself, "Smithy, that's the outfit for you."

After all, I wasn't doing much of anything and those dress blues were as sharp as could be. Couldn't wait to see myself in a set. So, I went down to Boston to join up.

Oh, and what a shock I got. I wasn't up to snuff with my weight and my height was also agin me. The doctor just smiled though.

"Son, stand on your tiptoes. You can always put on a few pounds."

I did, that was it. I was now a private in the rear ranks of the U.S. Marine Corps.

OK, let's jump ahead to 1942 and the battle of Midway. I was a corporal by then. My job was being a cook and my battle station was on a .50 caliber machine gun. I looked up in the air and saw all those meatballs buzzing around.

"Smithy," I said to myself, "you stood on your tiptoes to get into this lash-up. Must have been off your rocker."

One more thing. As I said when the war ended, I was on the island of Okinawa. My enlistment was up and I was still on active duty. COG (Convenience of the Government).

Well, I've always been good at making things. I had set up a new way for the men to wash their mess gear. A captain from a different company saw what I had done. He came over to me.

"Sergeant," he said, "I want to have you transferred into my company so you can set up one of those things for my people."

"Captain," I answered, "see that APA out in the harbor? I got a hundred and thirty points (more than enough for discharge) and when that ship leaves for the States, I better be on it or there'll be hell to pay."

I was on it.

Well, as you were. Back to '39. After my recruit training was over, I was sent to Hilton Head in South Carolina. That's a real swanky place now, but it wasn't anything like that back in '39.

At Hilton Head, we were putting together the 3rd Marine Defense Battalion. We had .30 and .50 caliber machine guns and three- and five-inch cannon. Never did get those five-inchers out of their wrappings. They were sent to Midway Island. We went along to set them up. Then we went to Pearl Harbor and did the same thing. I can remember one of the boys bitching like the devil about taking those five-inchers to Midway.

"What the hell are we doing out here? Even if we do go to war with Japan," he moaned, "there's no way the Jap Navy will get to Midway without being sunk."

MIDWAY! Hell, those guys were to get to *Oahu* without being detected!

Well, at Pearl, we were set up right near the Marine barracks with Hickam Field on our left. We had a good view of Battleship Row, and as I remember, December 7, '41 was a real clear day and we had the whole sneak attack on our fleet right in front of us.

Now, here is something that I find interesting. On November 26, the 3rd Defense Battalion went on full alert. We couldn't hit the sack. We had to keep moving with our helmets and full marching order packs on. Sometime very early on the twenty-seventh, I went into the galley to get a cup of coffee. So did our sergeant-major. I confronted him.

"Sergeant," I said, "what the hell is going on?"

"Well, you know that things are pretty testy between the U.S. and Japan," he answered. "We'd heard the Jap fleet was on maneuvers, but we really don't know where the hell they are."

Now, please note, nothing was said about a possible attack on Pearl, just that we were uneasy over the fact that we didn't know where the Japanese fleet was.

Anyway, about three o'clock that morning, the alert was called off. We never heard anything further about it.

December 7 was different. I had duty on the sixth, but had plans to go ashore the morning of the seventh. I was sleeping in when all of a sudden I was awakened by a god-awful racket. I looked out the window and saw all these planes buzzing around the fleet. I immediately saw the red balls painted on their wings.

"Holy Toledo," I said to myself, "the goddamned Japs are attacking us."

I grabbed my Springfield and ran outside to the area behind our barracks. There were five or six Marines from our battalion also out there. We were all blazing away at the Japanese planes with our Springfields. This wasn't as futile as it sounds. Our men were dead shots.

Those Japanese pilots were really excellent flyers. They were coming in very low, not only for strafing, but also for discharging their torpedoes.

All right. As you know, Pearl Harbor was really one fuck-up after another. Our plan was, in case of an attack, to have the Navy rush us the shells for our three-inchers.

Hell, no one stopped to think that we had the Army-style three-inchers. The Navy style was actually three and one-half inches, while the Army one was three inches flat.

So, the guns were all set up when the ammunition arrived. Christ Almighty, you should have heard the cursing. If they'd given us the right shells, we would have knocked those meatballs out of the sky.

When the second wave came over, we had our machine guns all set up. I had my eye on one plane that seemed to be coming right at me. A Marine captain was giving me the word.

"Lead that bastard in, Smitty. Hold your fire and lead him in." Finally he nodded his head.

"Let him have it, Smitty. You got him."

So I gave him a full blast of .50 caliber bullets. He started to smoke and he went down very near the corner of our hospital.

Now, don't get me wrong. Just about every machine gun we had was firing at him. His plane fell apart when it hit the ground.

There was one thing that impressed me like the devil. With all those planes going back and forth in a small area, none of them collided with each other. The Japanese surely had the best pilots they had up in the air on December 7.

Well, after the second wave left Pearl, everything was quiet for quite a while. Our battalion had a dozen or so casualties, but it was hard to tell if they had been hit by our fire or the Japanese. Many of our wounded had shrapnel wounds.

That night though one of the saddest things I saw during the whole war occurred. The U.S.S. *Enterprise* was just off Pearl. Some of our planes from the Big E radioed that they were coming in. But they said they were coming in from one direction and they came in from the opposite direction. We were expecting another wave of Japanese planes and the whole defense battalion was waiting for them. Of course they never came, but what did come were our own planes. Come what may, we were set up for anything. The night of the seventh, I was right there by my machine gun. I knew there was something above us, but I didn't know what.

So, this old gunny walked over to me. "Smitty," he said, "what are you standing around for?"

"Well, damn it, I'm waiting for orders."

"You've got your orders, start firing."

"Yup, but what will I be firing at?"

"I don't give a goddamn. Get some lead in the air and be fast about it."

So, hell, I started firing and so did all the other machine gunners in our battalion.

Now let me tell you something. We shot down our own planes that night, and it wasn't only our battalion. Just about all the other outfits were firing also. There was just one huge sheet of lead going up. I don't think a fly could have survived all that firing.

The next day I talked to one of the downed pilots. Of course we were apologetic as hell, but it didn't impress the fellows we'd shot down one iota.

"God Almighty," this naval commander said, "I've been in this man's Navy for a long time, but I've never seen such fire. The only problem was you were firing at your friends."

However, of the six to eight planes that were shot down, it seems to me most of the pilots were picked up. But I think someone might well have started the expression snafu right there at Pearl.

And it wasn't only the *Enterprise* planes Americans were firing at. With all the three-inch firing that the U.S. forces had set up during that long day, much of it had landed in Honolulu or on Ford Island. I am sure some of the civilians were wounded by shrapnel from American guns.

All right. We did take a beating on Pearl Harbor Sunday, something that made our big victory in June of '42 all the sweeter.

Well, this all happened half a century ago. After the war ended, we started a group called the Pearl Harbor Survivors Association. Here it is half a century after the attack and we have about eleven thousand members. To join you have to have been on the island of Oahu on the morning of the attack. Our commanding officer, Lt. Colonel Pepper, was out to sea at the time. He can't belong to the group. So be it.

PFC Doug Jones,
USMC, Marine Barracks, Oahu

◆

Oh, boy, can I remember Pearl Harbor! I was having some medical problems at the time and those damn Japanese planes just aggravated them. I was stationed at the Marine barracks over near Pearl then.

Well, in the first part of December of '41 I'd gone to sick call to have their doctor take a look at a small growth on my rectum. He did.

"Jones," he said, "you've got a cyst, all right. We can get that off in a second. You've also got a nasty case of hemorrhoids. Don't they bother you?"

"Oh, yes, they're quite tender."

"Well, I'll get rid of them and the cyst. We'll give you a local. Nothing to it."

So, they gave me a spinal. Remember, the Marine Corps has no medical department. The doctor was Navy and so was the corpsman helping him.

After they removed the cyst, they went to work on my piles. By now they were both laughing like the devil.

"Oh, Doctor," the corpsman said, "when you go after those hemorrhoids, don't hurt the Marine's brains."

They both laughed like all get out. I didn't.

Anyway, they sewed me all up and I must confess I didn't feel a thing. Then the corpsman spoke again.

"Doctor, did you notice this man is not circumcised? Why

don't we also give him a little clip job?" The doctor agreed, but, of course, he had to ask me.

"How about it, Jones? That foreskin can only get in your way. Let us take it off."

So, I figured, what the hell and I agreed.

Boy, you should have heard those two giving me the needle now, particularly the corpsman, who was talking to the doctor.

"We're going to really fix this bellhop up now," he said. "First one end and now the other. No matter which exit he uses, it is going to hurt."

OK, they bandaged up all my operations and sent me to a ward. The word spread fast. Everybody wanted to talk to the Marine who had both ends cut on.

So, on the morning of December 7, I was lying in bed reading the paper when I heard all this firing.

"What the hell is that noise?" someone yelled. Just then a corpsman came running into the ward.

"The Japs are bombing us, those bastards!"

By now I was up. I looked out the window. There was this Zero right over us, flying real low. He flew by fast. I had become chummy with this big sailor I'd met in the ward. The two of us rushed outside to see what we could see.

Just as we got outside another Zero came by. He was strafing everybody in sight. But the pilot had been hit and we could see he was going down. So, the big sailor jumped into this ditch and I jumped in on top of him. The stitches on my John Henry tore then and there.

As for the plane, it had crashed almost on top of us. I later heard it was the first Japanese plane shot down in the war. There I was, in a ditch, bleeding from my manhood, and right next to me is the first downed Japanese plane of the war.

And incidentally, I was later with the 4th Marines who went ashore in Japan shortly after the end of the war. So you could say my service went from Pearl Harbor to Japan in almost four years.

In any event, after the two waves of Japanese planes had finished their raiding, I went to the same doctor who had performed surgery on me a few days earlier.

My God, was he busy! There was no time for joking.

"Look at these men, Jones," he said. "You're walking around. Some of these poor lads are never going to walk around again. Take that thing of yours and wash it off thoroughly.

"Then start bathing it in hot salt water. If you keep doing that, it will eventually be fine." He was right.

Anyway I got a pitcher of cold water. I started giving each burn victim a cold drink. I could see right away that several of them weren't going to make it even though they were conscious.

Good God, I recognized one of them. His name was Hines and he was from a town near my home in Kansas. I had run against him in the quarter-mile race three times. He beat me by about a foot each time. We talked for a while and I moved on. I hope he got back to Kansas, but I doubt it. He was burned to a crisp.

Whatever, I never did get a Purple Heart, but I surely remember Pearl Harbor and that day when the Navy cut me in both holes.

To Hell with Babe Ruth

◈

By the mid-1930s baseball had taken over Japan. Its popularity knew no bounds. In 1934 Babe Ruth, Lou Gehrig, and an array of baseball stars toured the land of the Rising Sun. They played exhibition games from one end of Japan to the other.

There was also a substitute catcher on the trip named Moe Berg. A so-so ballplayer, the late Mr. Berg was a brilliant scholar. He could speak seven languages, including Japanese. Berg was officially the interpreter for the ball team. It was reported after the war started that Berg had also been a spy for the forerunner of the CIA while on the trip.

Anyway, where the American team went, they were ardently lionized, and when Ruth hit a "homer runner," the Japanese went berserk.

Five years after this Japanese trip, Lou Gehrig came down with the disease that is now known as Lou Gehrig's disease. He died on June 4, 1941.

A few months before Lou died, President Roosevelt, as the song says, left his troubles on the doorstep and went to the ball game. As always, the President was to throw out the opening day pitch for the Washington Senators in their game with the New York Yankees. FDR had been manager of the baseball team at Groton and loved the game.

Well, due to the international tensions there would be no pennant race in Japan in 1941. As a matter of fact, baseball of any kind was banned from Japan. It was a game for the decadent Americans, or so the Japanese said.

Be that as it may, back in 1934 all the players on the touring American team were presented with a very handsome medallion for giving so much joy to the Japanese people.

Now, let's go forward to the Japanese attack on Pearl Harbor. Just about all the Americans living within the continental limits of the United States were furious, but none more than Gehrig's widow, Eleanor. She mailed Lou's medal to FDR and told him the following.

"When we do bomb those creeps, give them back my beloved Lou's medallion. He wouldn't want it anymore and neither do I."

Now, let's say it was dropped over Tokyo and a Japanese retrieved it. If a 1933 Goudey baseball card of Gehrig sells for $1,500, what would a thank-you medallion with Gehrig's name inscribed on it and a short message about the trip to Japan be worth? Think about that.

Glen Turner, U.S.S. *California*

I was a real small-town boy, brought up in Windham, Minnesota, about 160 miles from Minneapolis. I knew our country had a large Navy, but I knew very little about it.

Nevertheless, I enlisted in that navy in September of 1940. Washington had started a draft at about the same time. Do you remember that song "Good-bye, Dear, I'll Be Back in a Year, 'Cause I'm in the Army Now"? As I was only nineteen at the time, I knew it would be a while before they'd get me, but I guess I just wanted to go into the Navy and not the Army. That was it.

So, after boot camp, I was sent out to Long Beach, California, where I went aboard the U.S.S. *California*. They did that in those days. You could go aboard a ship right after boot camp. I spent the next year or so aboard that battlewagon in the Pacific Fleet. While on the *California*, I was a fire control man.

Like all the other ships in the Pacific, the *California* mainly was in and out of Pearl Harbor. This meant that our liberty port was Honolulu. It was not my favorite city. Oh, it was all right if you were one of the group that hung around Hotel Street, but dogging around wasn't my speed.

The *California* did go back to Hunters Point in San Francisco to get our bottom scraped. Most of the crew was set to get fifteen days leave.

Then came the shocker. The Germans sank the U.S.S. *Reuben James*, an American destroyer. Wow, did the shit hit the fan! All leaves went out the window in a hurry. Before we knew it, we were back at Pearl, going out on weekly patrols.

On one of the cruises, we were maneuvering when all of a sudden they sounded General Quarters. I knew this was not a drill. It could be the real McCoy. All hands immediately went to their battle stations. The scuttlebutt told us an unidentified sub was in the area. Our escort destroyers let loose with some depth charges for a while. Then we were told to secure quarters. We went off the full alert.

This all happened before dawn on December 4, 1941. We thought nothing more about it, but hell, we must have been close to some Japanese ships, maybe their whole task force. So much for that.

We sailed back into Pearl the next day. I can remember exactly where they put us. We were tied up to a place called FE, just forward of the U.S.S. *Neosho*. We were quite close to the entrance to the channel between Ford Island and the Navy yard.

At this time, I had not been ashore for quite a while. But on the night of the sixth, they were having a band play-off at Pearl.

You see, each battleship had a band. All the bands were always arguing about which ship had the best band in the fleet. So with so many battleships in port, they decided to have a meeting of all the bands to see which one was the best.

This was great. They didn't play any military songs as I remember. Not in the play-off anyway. This was the period of the big bands. They played the songs of the Dorsey brothers, Glenn Miller, Benny Goodman, and Harry James, people like that.

And I mustn't forget Artie Shaw. He was the guy who was always marrying good-looking actresses.

Well, I must tell you, the music was great. I can't remember which band won, but it wasn't the one from the *California*.

But the real winners were the sailors. We just sat there and listened to all that good music and drank beer. It was the most fun I'd had since I left the States.

It all ended between ten and eleven. Some of my friends headed for "Hotel Street," but most of us went back to our ship. Someone brought up the General Quarters we'd had out to sea a few days earlier.

As for my watch, it was what we used to call pure chicken shit. I was dressed in my whites, those silly leggings, and a pistol belt. I had a .45 caliber automatic in the belt, but I don't really know what for. I sure as hell wasn't going to shoot anybody. My job was to make sure all the men had the uniform of the day on, their hats squared away right, and weren't smoking unless the smoking lamp was lit. You know, all that nitty-gritty crap.

Well, I had no sooner got to my position when I heard a loud explosion over on Ford Island. I looked up and I saw all these planes with that big meatball on their wings buzzing around us.

"Oh, my God," I said to myself, "the Japanese are attacking us."

I ran over to a phone to call the officer of the desk, but before I got there, they sounded General Quarters.

"This is not a drill," this guy kept announcing over and over.

So, I headed for my battle station as fast as I could. My station was a caged nest about 125 feet above the waterline. My job was to help direct the fire of our big guns. It was then that we took a torpedo on our port side. I knew we were in trouble.

Just forward of my station, there was a .50 caliber machine gun. There were two men breaking their backs trying to get the ammunition box open because they didn't have a key. Finally, they beat the lock off with something and after working like hell to get the box open, they found it empty. That gun didn't fire all morning.

The same thing happened to our big guns. There had been complaints from the local citizens about having so many high explosives lying around. It seems that our big shells had been put below decks to satisfy the good people of Honolulu.

To really foul things up, that torpedo we had taken had knocked out our electric systems. The only way to get the shells above decks was to form a human line, each sailor handing the shells up to the guy above him. It was just like the song, you know, "Praise the Lord and Pass the Ammunition."

In the meantime, our ship was beginning to list more and more on the port side. We all felt sure as hell we were going over on our side. But we weren't the only battlewagon in trouble. The *Okie* was already on its side with hundreds of sailors trying to slide down the side above the water. They wanted to get to that oily water just to stay alive.

The *West Virginia* was also taking a dreadful pounding. We didn't know, but I guess her skipper was already dead. Inboard of here was the *Tennessee*. It looked as if most of her guns were blasting away.

It was the same for the *Maryland*. One of these two ships had recently had her firepower greatly modernized. Those two were firing away with everything they had.

As for the *Arizona*, that was a horse of a different color. I wasn't looking in their direction when it happened, so I didn't see it explode, but I sure heard it. My God, what a racket. It sounded like Armageddon and I guess it was just that for hundreds of lads aboard her. Almost immediately, the harbor started to really fill with oil. Beautiful Pearl was being turned into a dung heap.

Back to the *California*. Things were getting desperate. We knew scores of sailors had been lost when the *Okie* had capsized. It looked like we might be doing the same thing.

To make matters worse, inboard from us was the *Neosho*, a fleet tanker that was loaded with high-test gasoline. If that went up you would have had the fourth of July a hundred times over.

So, the word came through, "Abandon ship! Abandon ship!" I went to the fo'c'sle on the starboard side. There were launches there to take the crew off, but the place was mobbed.

"Hell," I said to myself, "I'm a good swimmer. I'll dive in."

So I did. I started to swim over to Ford Island. Everything was going great until I got halfway there. Then I started to swim into oil. I don't know if you've ever run into oil when swimming, but try not to. It is murder. I must have looked like the creature from the deep lagoon when I crawled ashore. I promptly started to puke my lungs out getting rid of that damn oil.

Anyway, sick or not, the second wave of Japanese planes was still buzzing around and strafing everyone they could see. The war had definitely started on the Japanese terms. It was not a healthy spot to be in.

O.K. There was a baseball diamond right where I had crawled ashore. I got the bright idea to hide in one of the dugouts. It worked like a charm. I was safe and sound until the Japanese left.

When I realized they weren't coming back I started to wander around in a daze. I went into a garage where I got some gasoline and tried to wash the oil off my skin.

Hell, it was hopeless. At the time, all I had on were my skivvie drawers, but no one gave a damn. Then I spotted some dungarees hanging on a line. I grabbed them and put them on in a hurry.

Next I headed for the mooring where I had left the *California*. By this time our officers realized she wasn't going over on her side unless there was a third wave coming over. A CPO was yelling for volunteers to come back aboard to fight the fires, so back I went.

In the meantime, I was still barefoot. I sure as the devil didn't want to fight fires with no shoes on, so I went over to the port side to try to find my shoes. Sure enough, there they were just where I had left them.

Now came the most gruesome work detail I had while in the bloody Navy. I was put with the group to remove the bodies of the men who had been passing up the ammunition. I hadn't known any of these men and even if I had, I couldn't recognize them. They were in bits and pieces.

After that, it was back to fighting fires. At least we were winning that battle. By sundown, I was really beat down to my socks. I was sitting on the quarterdeck when a detail started to lower our colors.

"Oh, no," I moaned out loud, "don't strike our colors." The

day had been too much for me. I cried like a baby. I should have known better.

You see, when they started to lower our colors, I thought we were surrendering. I was in a daze. What I'd forgotten was that when you are in port, even during a war, you always raise the flag at 0800 and take it down at sunset. Of course, when you are out to sea, it flies twenty-four hours a day. When I realized what was going on, I felt a lot better.

Well, so far as I can see, the Pearl Harbor attack was a snafu from start to finish. One of the most memorable to me was my missing muster the morning of the eighth. This caused my family to get a telegram stating that I was missing in action and presumed dead. Good God, this caused all kinds of grief back in Windham, Minnesota. I was out to sea on a different ship (U.S.S. *Astoria*) by the time my family found out I was alive.

After the *Astoria* went down off Guadalcanal (August 9, 1942), I was picked up by a destroyer (U.S.S. *Bagley*).

This time, I was given survivor's leave and went back home. My mother showed me all the sympathy cards they had received concerning my death. I started to laugh. I looked over at Mother. She had tears in her eyes. She looked at me and shook her head.

"Glen," she said, "there was nothing funny about it, nothing funny at all."

Well, the years have gone by. It is now a half century since that Sunday morning of hell. But it sure is hard to forget.

Faint Praise

To every veteran of the Pearl Harbor attack that I visited with, the Japanese aircraft obtained a complete and stunning victory on December 7, 1941. But how did the Japanese military feel about it?

To begin with, Admiral Yamamoto was crushed. Above all, he wanted our carriers. None were there. Yamamoto was totally against the war. His feelings were certainly not altruistic in any way. He would have been delighted to destroy any country that stood in the way of his beloved Japan. But he had spent several years in the United States. He knew the awesome industrial power of the country. He did not share the belief of many of his countrymen that Americans were lacking in fortitude.

In short, he did not think Japan could win a war with the U.S. The best they could hope for was some kind of a no-win, no-lose situation, and even that was iffy.

Above all, Yamamoto was the leading proponent of the theory that Japan must declare war on the U.S. before the attack on Pearl. He was completely supported by the emperor on the declaration.

Or so he said. Yet, he was the sponsor of the attack. Surely he knew that surprise was an absolute necessity for its success.

Well, Yamamoto may have been the real sponsor of the Pearl Harbor attack, but he was thousands of miles away when it occurred. What did the pilots who did the job think of their foes down below?

Here is a direct response to a question from the emperor as reported in *God's Samurai*, the life story of Mitsuo Fuchida, the flight commander of the Japanese Air Force at Pearl.

Emperor Hirohito—"What was the initial reaction of the Americans (to the attack)?"

Fuchida—"Two minutes after our first bombs were dropped, we received very heavy bursts of antiaircraft. In truth, we were surprised that the Americans could recover so quickly."

And so it goes.

Marty Friedman

◆

Mr. Friedman was a New York City boy. He was born there in 1912. After the Japanese attack he decided to join the U.S. Marines.

Actually Marty was slightly over the maximum age limit but he had said he wanted to be a Marine correspondent. They were something the Corps was short on.

In his late twenties he went through the Parris Island recruit camp affectionately being called "Pop" by his fellow boots. Marty was awarded the Purple Heart and the Bronze Star on Okinawa. Take it over, Martin.

So, you want to know where I was when the Japanese attacked the U.S. at Pearl Harbor. OK. I was working for Warner Brothers, going all over the country to check out shows. It was quite common to tie in a reasonably short live show with a film on the same bill. Our job was either to forget a show or recommend that Warner's buy it.

And that's why on December 7, '41 I was driving between Cleveland and Sandusky in the state of Ohio. Another Warner's employee was with me.

Remember, there were no superhighways then. It was a lousy drive. We had the car radio on. I think my companion was half

68

asleep. A news report broke into the regular programming. I can recall almost word for word what he said. Here it is:

"We are interrupting this program for a special report. At this very moment Japanese airplanes are attacking the United States Naval Base at Pearl Harbor on the island of Oahu in the Hawaiian Islands. Stay tuned to this program for further developments."

Wow! I almost drove off the side of the road. I'd been to Pearl Harbor. Oh, it was so beautiful. When you'd go to the movies, you'd frequently see news shots of bombed-out areas in Europe. I could imagine what Pearl Harbor must look like. Then my friend woke up.

"For Christ's sake, Marty, why have we stopped?" I told him what I'd heard on the radio. Oh, boy, did he let go with a string of curses.

Whatever, we decided to go on to Sandusky, see the show, then go back to Cleveland to determine what we'd do next.

So, the show did go on, but you could feel the electricity going through the crowd. The cast seemed to want to say their lines as quickly as possible and get it over with. We could hear a radio blaring backstage.

Like everyone else, when the show was over, we headed for a radio. I can't remember what we thought of the show but who cared.

So, that was it. But I'll never forget that when one of the most earth-shaking events of this century occurred, me, Marty Friedman, was on my way to Sandusky, Ohio.

James Benham, Lt. Junior Grade, U.S.S. *Farragut*

◈

"Going back, going back,
Going back to Nassau Hall.
Going back, going back
To the best old place of all."
—Old Princeton Song

When Jim Benham enrolled at Princeton University, the last thing on his mind was a six-year cruise in the U.S. Navy. But by the time he graduated, Hitler was about to send his troops into Poland. Nothing was to be the same again.

Jim went on active duty in the U.S. Navy in 1940. By the first part of '41 he was an ensign aboard the U.S.S. *Farragut* in the Pacific Fleet at Pearl Harbor. From then until the end of World War II he was almost constantly at sea, figuring in most of the major sea battles of the Pacific war. While he spent a short tour of duty aboard a CV aircraft carrier (the U.S.S. *Randolph*), he was mostly a tin can sailor. He was separated from the Navy as a lieutenant commander at the end of '45.

Jim then carved out a very successful career for himself as an advertising executive in New York City. He is now retired and living with his wife of forty years in Fairfield County, Connecticut. At seventy-five he is still one of the better golfers at the challenging Wee Burn course, one of the toughest in the state of Connecticut.

Jim Benham is one of the two people I already knew when I

started writing this book. It was through Jim that I got involved with the Pearl Harbor Survivors Association. This was essential to my completing *"This Is No Drill!"* Jim, I salute you. Take over, Mr. Benham.

When I graduated from Princeton in 1939, I took some meaningless jobs. One was with the New York *Daily News* where I was a newsboy. This was exciting as hell to a young guy but hardly what I expected after Princeton.

In the meantime at the end of August it all started. I was visiting a college buddy in Bethlehem, Pennsylvania, for the weekend when Hitler sent his hobnail-booted boys into Poland. Like everyone else my age I had been brought up on stories about the Great War from the older generation. I felt we'd be involved again. It was just a matter of time.

So, later that year another Princeton pal got ahold of me.

"Jim," he said, "the Navy has announced a new program that seems as attractive as hell to me. It is called the V-7 Program. It is only for college grads. After you join up, you take a thirty-day cruise aboard a battleship.

"Then you spend ninety days at midshipmen's school and you come out an ensign in the U.S. Naval Reserves. If America does get involved in the war going on in Europe, you'll go in as an officer, which is a hell of a lot nicer than being a gob. Besides, the dolls will love you in those dress-white uniforms."

Hell, that was the answer to a maiden's prayer, as we used to say. It sounded great to me.

So, I enlisted. At first I was an apprentice seaman. You know, with the white hat and the bell-bottom trousers. They put six hundred or so of us aboard the U.S.S. *Texas*. This was in addition to the regular crew. First, we headed for Guantánamo in Cuba and after that the Panama Canal.

And what a spot Panama City was in those days! It was there that I found out what good liberty meant in the peacetime Navy.

Can you imagine six hundred guys, recently out of college, being turned loose in a place like Panama with their crazy bell-bottoms and a few bucks in their jeans? Wow! We made a wreck of the place, but we sure left a lot of dough there! Don't know if any of those brand-new sailors picked up the clap, but it was a possibility.

The captain of the *Texas* was a man named Barbie. He ended up with a big job when MacArthur returned to the Philippines in '44.

Barbie was a good man. He wanted to put together a newspaper on the cruise so we could have a souvenir of our entrance into the Navy. I was one of the eight men he asked to do the job, which gave me an opportunity to get to really know him.

And, you know, the Navy kept an up-to-date evaluation on each man. Working on that paper probably is why I was made communications officer when I went aboard the *Farragut* later on at Pearl.

We got back to the States and were told we'd be going aboard the U.S.S. *Illinois* for midshipmen's school in a few weeks.

Well, you know that old expression about the Service, "Hurry up and wait"? It was three or four months before they were ready for us.

Shortly after my officer's training started, we got the word Roosevelt had called up the Naval Reserve. If we didn't hack it at midshipmen's school, instead of going home, we'd go to the fleet as a gob.

I passed with flying colors. Now I was an active duty ensign. I said my preference was the Pacific Fleet on a destroyer and that's just where they sent me.

My ship was the U.S.S. *Farragut*, a 1934 destroyer then at Pearl Harbor. Along with another Reservist, a great guy named Donald Sleeper, I headed west. When we got to Pearl, we received a bit of a shock.

You see, we were the first two Reserve officers to go aboard the *Farragut*. All the other officers were Annapolis men who had sweated for four years to get their commissions. Don and I were ninety-day wonders. We were as popular as a turd in a punch bowl.

But as the time wore on, all that Reserve versus regular crap went out the window. I did point out that while I had all the respect in the world for the Naval Academy, Harvard and Princeton, where Don and I had gone, were not exactly high schools. In a few months, everything was fine.

Now, let me tell you about our captain, Lt. Commander George Porter Hunter. The skipper was from Massachusetts and was a real gentleman. He never did make admiral, which surprised me, because he was everything an outstanding officer should be.

OK. Outside of his family, he had two compelling passions, the U.S. Navy and golf, not necessarily in that order. Every chance he had, he would be on the links.

By the time I got to know him I had been made communications officer. Every now and then Mr. Hunter would check in to make sure everything was under control. On one of these visits he mentioned that he had a golf date the next day.

"Gee, sir," I said, "you must really love golf, the amount you play."

"I sure do, Mr. Benham," he answered. "How about you? Do you play?"

"Yes, sir, I love the game. But my clubs are back in New York City."

"Hell, Jim, get them expressed out here."

This was the peacetime Navy. We worked hard, but we were also supposed to have some fun. I told the skipper I would do that right away. Then I thought of my friend Don. I told the skipper that Sleeper also loved golf.

"That's great," he said. "Tell Mr. Sleeper also to get his sticks sent out here. I like to have all my young officers playing golf. It is real relaxing."

That was it. Once or twice a week when we were in port, Mrs. Hunter would drive up to our ship. Sleeper and I would pack our clubs over our shoulders and follow the skipper down the gangway into his wife's car and head for Waikiki.

I had another pal from midshipmen's school named Sid Biddle. He was also on a destroyer but in a different group from me. When he was out to sea, I would be in port and vice versa.

So, we decided to chip in and buy a secondhand car. We put in fifty bucks each and picked up a four-door Chevy convertible.

Wow! I could drive all over the island with the top down. And from time to time I'd drive near Hotel Street, particularly if I had a young lady with me. If some sailors from the *Farragut* were standing in line, I'd honk at them. They'd get a big boot out of this and so would I.

Oh, yes, one more thing I can remember about the car. I had it one day in October, I think it was a Sunday morning. I had a World Series game on the car radio. The game was coming in from Brooklyn clear as crystal.

And I'll bet you can remember the game. It was the one where Mickey Owen dropped the third strike and Tommy Henrich went to first base safely. There were two outs at the time and Hugh Casey was pitching for the Dodgers. Then the Yankees exploded. Keller, Joe D., Dickey, all those Yankee sluggers got hits. It put New York in the catbird seat, as Red Barber used to say. I later heard Hugh Casey committed suicide. Don't know if that game was the reason though.

Well, as you can see, the peacetime Navy was good duty, especially for a young officer on liberty, with the top down, in his car, and a suntan on his face and those snappy white uniforms. With that setup a few years earlier back at Princeton, I would have made out like a bandit.

But it wasn't all fun and games. Yes, the officers had most weekends and Wednesdays off when we were in port. However, we could be out to sea for weeks at a time and that was basically real work.

Anyway, it all began to change in the fall of '41. We started to get all these communications about how dangerous the situation was getting with the Japanese.

Remember, I was communications officer and when I was on duty, I would get all the wires and what have you first. There were several messages telling us to beware of a sneak attack from the Japanese. It seems they had pulled off a surprise attack on the Russians at Port Arthur in '04.

We received several warnings from Washington all right, but we never did get the one telling us to get off our dead ass, that the Japanese could be coming to Pearl Harbor.

Don't get me wrong. All the officers I knew expected we'd go to war against Japan and that it would probably start off with a surprise air raid.

But at Pearl? Never! Too far away. The Philippines, Singapore, or even Indonesia, where all the oil is.

Come to think of it, though, there was one thing that did happen on a cruise we had around the end of November. I got a message and was told to decipher it and get it to the skipper on the double. Here's what it said.

"This is no drill. You should meet up with task force whatever at such and such a place and immediately. Go at flank speed."

Hell, we had never been at flank speed since I had been on the *Farragut*. This was serious business all right.

Of course we complied, but nothing ever happened. It did put us to thinking. We certainly knew that the peace talks at Washington were going nowhere. But I still don't think any of us expected a Japanese strike at Pearl.

So, back to Pearl we went. For the weekend of December 6-7 I was given the duty. It was my watch as we used to say. This meant that I would be the only officer on board the night of December 6. All the unmarried officers were kicking the gong around ashore, while the married officers were with their families.

I dined alone in the officers' mess, watched the traditional Saturday night movie, and waited for the enlisted men to come back from Pearl. The OD had to be there when the Whale Boat came back because some of the men would occasionally be pretty well beaten up. Others would be sent back by the Shore Patrol. Our men seemed to be a particularly hard-drinking bunch of salts.

On this night, though, everything was under control. I went back to my quarters and started to read a book. Then I dozed off.

Around 2400 hours the gangway watch banged on my door.

"Mr. Benham," he was yelling, "Mr. Sleeper is at the officers' Club and would like a Whale Boat so he can return to the ship. He is with two officers from other ships in our nest."[1]

No trouble here. I knew Don would be in good shape. He usually was. After he was on board, I went back to sleep. It was about 0200 when I got my second call from the watch. This was another story.

It seems that one of our senior bachelor officers also wanted a Whale Boat. This guy was just about the most popular officer aboard. He was a regular officer who loved liberty. As a matter of fact he had made it into a fine art. Could he tie one on! Wow!

Now, don't get me wrong. He was an outstanding officer, but when he played, he played. If it was two o'clock, the odds were that he was probably three sheets to the wind. I would need help this time.

Damn it, I was right! With the help of the watch we got this guy down to his quarters, bouncing him off the bulkheads as we went. I returned to my sack to really cork off.

I woke up around 0730 and started to move around. As the OD I had to be on deck for colors at 0800. All of a sudden the chief quartermaster comes tearing into my quarters.

"Mr. Benham, Mr. Benham, get on the deck on the double!"

I knew this was an emergency. The men just didn't talk to the officers that way. So I put on my silk bathrobe and dashed out.

My God, I can see all these planes buzzing around our battleship like so many gnats around a lightbulb. "Holy shit," I mut-

---

[1]When four ships were tied up together, it was called a nest.

tered, "those are meatballs! This is the real McCoy!" I dashed back to my quarters, quickly put on my combat gear, and went topside. As the communications officer, my battle station was on the bridge with the captain.

But where is the captain? Hell, he's on the first hole at Waikiki. The officer whom we had been bouncing off the walls is in command.

Well, as I said, he was a real officer. Hangover or no hangover, he showed up ready for duty.

"Tell the men to fire up the boilers. We've got to get under way as soon as possible," he yelled.

You see, in our nest there were four tin cans. One of them had to be ready for immediate action at all times. On December 7 it was the *Monaghan*. Her boilers were ready to roll. She sailed out into the harbor. They spotted a midget submarine. If I am not mistaken, the *Monaghan* simply rammed the sub, cutting it in half and sending it to the bottom.

A few minutes later I was looking at the *Arizona* when I heard this tremendous explosion. Oh, my God, a huge sheet of flames raced into the air. There were bodies everywhere and oil was quickly filling the harbor with gook. It was a horrifying sight, one I will never forget.

Later, one of our battleships, the *Nevada*, decided to make a run for the open sea. But as I noticed her, so did the Japanese. It would have been a tremendous coup if they could have sunk her right at the entrance to the harbor. This would have put Pearl out of business for months. And the Japanese pilots went after her from all sides. The captain of the *Nevada*, realizing what they were up to, pulled his ship out of the way and beached her. At least he got her away from the entrance to the harbor.

In the meantime, the Japanese were bombing and strafing everything in sight. They were coming in real low. Hell, we could see the faces of the bastards. And there were those big meatballs, looking down on us.

By this time our boilers were working. We could elevate our five-inchers, so we fired them at the Japanese. It turned out that many of our shells were defective. Some of the good ones landed at Pearl City. There were some sixty-two or so civilians killed during the attack. Many of the dead had to be killed by friendly fire.

Well, when we got going, we went out of the channel, looking for the Japanese fleet. I think there was a cruiser with us, maybe the *Honolulu*. Thank God we didn't find the Japanese as they could have blown us out of the water. We stayed out a day or so, then we returned to Pearl.

My God, what a sight awaited us! Pearl Harbor had been a beautiful body of water. Narrow little channel and a great big harbor.

Well, the harbor was full of this disgusting oil. I mean it was everywhere! And it stank. Plus, you could see all those ships in varying degrees of damage. Beautiful Pearl. They had turned it into a ships' graveyard.

So, who is waiting for us on the dock? Our golfing skipper, that's who. And a couple of our other married officers who had been ashore during the attack. We picked them up and also some supplies. Then we were off again, hoping for a crack at the Japanese.

It took a while, but we did get it at the battle of the Coral Sea. We lost the U.S.S. *Lexington* there, but I believe they lost a carrier also. I have the *Farragut*'s battle flag hanging on the wall at my home. After the Coral Sea battle, we nailed their ass at Midway in June.

OK. Did the Japanese really gain anything from Pearl? All our battleships, except the *Arizona* and the *Oklahoma*, were back in action before the war was over.

What the Japanese did also with the attack was unite the American people in the war that had been forced upon them. Of course they now say their attack was in self-defense. And to that I say, "Baloney!"

Groton and Harvard in Tokyo

Joseph Grew became the U.S. Ambassador to Japan in 1932. He was typical of the "old shoe" type ambassador. If Gilbert and Sullivan had been around at the time, they could have penned a catchy tune about Mr. Grew being the epitome of a modern ambassador.

While Grew was picked for the Tokyo job by Herbert Hoover, there was no chance of his losing the job when FDR became President. After all they were old school chums from Groton and Harvard. Roosevelt was one who liked being on a first-name basis with his friends. One can easily imagine him calling Grew in Tokyo and saying, "Well, Joseph, how are things over there?"

However, there was a lot more to Mr. Grew than the old school tie. After graduating from Harvard (1902), he had taken a trip around the world. It was a fashionable thing to do. He shot a tiger in Amoy, China. This greatly impressed the then American President Teddy Roosevelt (another Groton and Harvard man) to such an extent that he approved Grew's appointment to the U.S. Foreign Service.

From then on he served all over the globe until he landed in Japan. He was the first U.S. career foreign service officer to be made ambassador to a major power.

The right honorable Mr. Grew stood over six feet tall, had bushy eyebrows, and a well-kept mustache. He was greatly helped by his wife who was a granddaughter of the Commodore Perry who had opened Japan to the world in 1853. She had spent her youth in Japan, knew the language well, and had an entrée to the leading families in Japan, no mean trick for an American.

Ambassador Grew took it onto himself to try to explain Americans to the Japanese and vice versa. He was the first American to hear about the coming attack.

There was a party at the Peruvian embassy. The embassy's Japanese interpreter had too much to drink. He exclaimed, "The American fleet will be destroyed!"

The Peruvian ambassador kept pumping his interpreter, trying to find out when this would happen. The Peruvian finally came to the conclusion it would be Pearl Harbor. He quickly told Mr. Grew. This was in early 1941.

Grew immediately informed Washington of the Pearl Harbor rumor. Washington in turn wired Admiral Kimmel on Oahu. Kimmel just wasn't in the mood to accept it.

"We are hearing a rumor a week on when and where the Japanese will attack us," stated Kimmel. "It is usually the Philippines or a British colony like Singapore. But Pearl Harbor? That is highly unlikely. The Japanese want oil. They'll be going toward Indonesia. That's in the other direction."

Well, for the rest of 1941 the information on a coming Japanese attack came from every direction. There did not seem to be any doubt but that Japan would attack the U.S. somewhere, but when or where still remained a question mark.

Anyway, in 1942 Ambassador Grew was repatriated to the United States. During his decade in Japan he probably did more than any other person to keep the peace between the Japanese Empire and the United States. He was held in high regard by both the Japanese and American foreign services. If anyone rated a "job well done," it was Joseph Grew. Or put another way.

"Blessed are the peacemakers."—Matthew, V; 9

So be it.

The Unluckiest Sailor
in the Pacific Fleet

Michael Zuvaun had to have been one of the unluckiest guys in the United States Navy. He drank too much of that Hotel Street booze one night and came aboard his ship, the U.S.S. *Ellet*, ready to fight everyone aboard. He received a deck court-martial and ten days on piss and bunk (bread and water).

The only problem was the *Ellet* was so small it had no brig. Instead of giving him ten days of extra duty, the exec on the *Ellet* arranged to have Michael serve his time on another ship that did have a brig. The other ship turned out to be the U.S.S. *Arizona*.

When the attack came a kind Marine guard went out of his way to see that Zuvaun was released and Michael hightailed it topside. But there was no place to hide on the *Arizona*. Zuvaun was killed and so probably was the Marine guard.

On the Old Fall River Line

◆

In April of 1991 they had a large gathering of the Pearl Harbor Survivors Association in Fall River, Massachusetts. These veterans came from all over New England, New York, and New Jersey. These are the states that make up District One in this organization.

My main reason for attending this meeting dates back almost two years to when I started my interviewing. I was still wrestling with a question that I still couldn't answer to my own satisfaction. In short, who was really at fault for allowing the United States military forces to be so completely surprised at Pearl Harbor on December 7, 1941?

I was fortunate enough to put together a group of five Pearl Harbor veterans in a hotel room at the reunion. I let my tape recorder run for the better part of an hour while we all just chewed the fat. Once again, it would appear that these five men were quite knowledgeable on the shocking event that took place on the island of Oahu half a century ago. I opened up the session with a question.

"Gentlemen," I stated, "I'd like your opinion on why this country was so completely caught with our pants down by the Japanese?"[Where I open up with a dash a different man is talking.] My first answer was both straight to the point and also revealing.

—Because we were bloody dopes.

—Amen to that! We all agree with you. But I think there is a lot more to it.

—There certainly is. Roosevelt wanted us in that bloody war. Maybe he was right. But he's on record as saying, "Japan must fire the first shot."

—And how about the last-ditch telegram he sent to the emperor of Japan? The one the Japanese deliberately let get bogged down in red tape. It wasn't delivered until well after the war had begun.

—Oh, the emperor, they called him the Mikado. Do you remember that show on Broadway, *The Hot Mikado*? Hell, we used to laugh at Japan in those days.

—Well, speaking of telegrams, the famous one sent to Pearl Harbor by General Marshall. It arrived after the bombs started dropping. If only Marshall had put through a person-to-person call to Short or Kimmel, we could have given those Nips a warm reception.

—Then I heard they couldn't disturb Marshall; he was out for his Sunday horseback ride.

—I'll say, but if you talk to every member at this meeting, you'll get stories that are hard to believe. You know, like they're being taken off full alert or General Quarters. Hell, there are so many of those tales you'd think someone wanted to make it convenient for the Japs.

—And the stories about the Navy putting the ammunition down below decks, making it difficult to get it in a hurry.

—One sailor told me that they had to do that because the good citizens of Honolulu didn't want ammunition lying around. For Christ's sake, we were their protection!

—Well, here's something that really pissed me off. Those vultures back in Washington couldn't wait to put the blame on someone. So they fired Kimmel and Short. The only thing those two were guilty of was not getting the straight poop from Washington.

—Shit, there always has to be a fall guy and Kimmel and Short were easy pickings.

—I'll tell you another reason for the great snafu. I don't think any of the brass back in the States had any respect for the Japs.

They couldn't believe they could come seven or eight thousand miles and deliver such a crushing blow. And, as a matter of fact, neither did those of us stationed on Oahu.

—That's true. I can't imagine anyone in his right mind not realizing the Japs had to make a move. But, Pearl? Never! Indochina, the Philippines, Singapore, any number of places. But not Oahu. Too far away and too risky.

—OK, you asked us who was responsible for the success of the attack on Pearl. Obviously, it was the Japanese. After all, the U.S. didn't bomb Pearl Harbor. But what a price the Nips paid!

—But look where they are now! They want to do with dollars what they couldn't do with bullets.

—OK, but we sure helped them get there.

—We all know that, but let's get back to December 7. Do you guys remember where General Short's office was? Hell, it was right next to where that CIA guy was. Or whatever we called the spooks in those days. The word I got was those cloak and dagger cats were sending constant information back to Washington but not telling Kimmel or Short anything. Why keep the brass in the field in the dark?

—That's it. The scoop those intelligence birds were sending back to the States would get lost in that bureaucratic maze they had back then.

—But you know, all you had to do was read the papers. The Japanese were the third partner in the Axis Powers. That triumvirate was living high on the hog. The Italian army wasn't much but the Germans seemed invincible. England was hanging in there by the skin of its teeth. The Krauts were closing in on Moscow. It was looking good for the Axis.

—Absolutely. And those Krauts were the masters of Europe all right. That's why the Japanese military leaders were so high on the Germans. The Nips wanted to take over the world all the way to India. They could eventually lock up with the Nazis.

—That's right. They wanted to control their so-called Greater East Asia Co-Prosperity Sphere. The only problem was they jumped the gun on the Germans. Hitler knew he'd have to deal with the Americans eventually, but he felt that would be down the road a few years.

—Well, the Japanese certainly forced Hitler's hand. But I still think that tyrant was crazy to declare war on the U.S.

OK. In examining my seventy plus interviews I came up with the following concerning my question, "Why was the American military caught with their pants down at Pearl Harbor?" This represents a very large majority, if not all, of the answers I received.

"The problem," I was told, "was simply a lack of or a breakdown of, communications between Pearl Harbor and Washington." It was as simple as that.

Now, Why Did They Do That?

◆

In mid-1941 the eyes of most Americans were on Europe. While no one wanted to see another AEF going "over there" à la 1918, a rather large majority most assuredly did not want to see a German victory. Doing business with an all-conquering Nazi government was enough to scare the daylights out of anyone.

Asia was another story. The Sino-Japanese War had been going on for years. It would probably go on for another ten. Even if Japan did win, how could they possibly control a land as huge as China? There just wasn't much interest in a war in Asia. Europe, that was the big show.

All citizens did not feel that way. An American senator from Wisconsin, named Wiley, was very interested in the Asian situation. He was astounded to find out that many large Japanese firms were withdrawing large sums from American banks.

At a time when the Japanese government and Japanese businessmen should have been depositing big to cover the large shipments of oil and military equipment going to Japan, they were quietly withdrawing funds. Wiley found this very odd and he made many comments about it.

Out on the West Coast two very successful Japanese businessmen had succeeded in getting temporary memberships in a rather exclusive golf club. It wasn't easy. Both of them had become smitten with the game of golf. They played every chance they could.

A few days after the Pearl Harbor attack the member who had

sponsored the two Japanese businessmen went over to the club to find out how his friends were making out.

"Oh, it was very strange," he was told. "About two weeks ago they both came over, resigned, and picked up all their stuff. They told us they had been called home suddenly. I guess they sailed the same day. They were surely in a big hurry."

What did they know?

Eric Ferguson

◆

Eric is one of the country's leading authorities on the Big Band Era in the United States. The two of us had a long discussion on those days of Vaughn Monroe racing with the moon. Then I asked him where he was on December 7, 1941. He answered me.

I was in West Orange, New Jersey. A bunch of us had a little six-piece band. We had gone to Eric Langmire's apartment to practice our routines. I was on the clarinet and Eric was the drummer. Eric was a little older than the rest of us. He'd been bitching about the peacetime draft.

"You guys have a few more years before they get you, but I'll probably get caught next spring. I'm already registered."

Eric was right. I was eighteen at the time. But just a year before a bunch of us had been talking about crossing into Canada and joining the RCAF. But Dad found out about it.

"Eric," he said, "don't forget that you were born in Scotland and you're still not an American citizen. Once you get over there, you might have trouble getting back in here." He was right.

Well, I think we were playing "Chattanooga Choo-Choo" when the phone rang. I can't remember who it was that answered the phone, but he quickly told us we were at war.

As I'm sure you realize, that was the end of our jam session. One of us spoke up.

"Hey," he said, "has any of you ever known a Jap from Japan?" I knew I had not. It turned out not a one of us could say yes.

Well, there was one thing we could all say. After that sneak punch those Japanese had killed all those American lads with, they were dog shit to us.

Our band was actually six young men. We all went into the service and all but one came back. It took a lot of doing, but we made those Japanese pay for what they did at Pearl.

Corporal James Noren

My father was a carpenter. When the war with Spain came along, he immediately enlisted in the Navy. He was on his way to Cuba when the war ended. All this was long before I was born. When I did come along, our family was living in Norfolk, Virginia, but not for long. When I was six years old, Dad moved us lock, stock, and barrel to Maryland, right outside of Washington. That's where I grew up.

I graduated from high school in 1939. I didn't want to be a burden to my parents so I figured I'd put a couple of years in the Army and perhaps learn something I could use in later life. I went over to the recruiting office at Pennsylvania Avenue, Northwest, in D.C. and joined up. I can still remember the date; it was August 4 in '39. This was just a few weeks before Hitler went into Poland.

First I went to Fort Slocum for basic training. When I completed this, they asked me where I'd like to go for duty: I figured Hawaii sounded great. I'd put in two to three years in Honolulu, come back home, and get a good job. It sounded good, but Tojo had other plans.

Well, Air Corps life started out just fine. After a month at Fort Slocum, I sailed out of New York City but not before I'd spent a few days at the World's Fair. This was a real treat!

All right, I believe the ship was called the *Leonard Wood*. From New York City we went down to the Panama Canal and up to San Francisco.

And lo and behold, they were also having a World's Fair in San Francisco. It was a lot smaller than the one in New York City, but quite good.

So, my next stop was the island of Oahu. We landed there in October of 1939. They were building Hickam Field at the time. We were quartered in Army tents and given casual duty. I don't know if you ever did casual duty, but it can be great or real chicken shit. Mine was great.

Our job was easy. We'd take the ferry over to Ford Island at about 8:30 in the morning. They had some barracks over at Ford. We'd strip the beds each day and come back to the Andrew Young Hotel.

Oh, and let me tell you something. My wife and I went back to Pearl about four or five years ago. I took her to the Andrew Young. It sure had changed!

Hell, they had turned the Andrew Young into office buildings. It took quite a pasting during the attack in '41. They have left many of the bullet holes in the walls just as they were shot there fifty years ago. The people seem to love to show this to the tourists. The day we were there they were showing it to some Japanese. They were just nodding their heads and mumbling, "Ah so, ah so." Then they'd shake their heads up and down.

Anyway, the Army finished Hickam in February of '40. Our unit was one of the first groups to be stationed there. Of course everything was sparkling new. And our commanding officer was going to keep it that way. As a matter of fact, we thought he was a little squirrelly about it all.

All right, we were flying B-17s and 18s. I was a chief radio operator and a gunner. Our whole crew was trained to be experts in our jobs.

But we couldn't do what we were supposed to do. Our commanding officer was bound to have our base the most beautiful base in the U.S. Army. Our flight engineers, radio operators, gunners, and all the enlisted men were constantly on base work details. Hell, we were gardeners, not airmen. Our commanding officer was a real problem.

His name was Brigadier-General P. P. Frank. We used to call him Place of Prison Frank. He was really old Army if anyone was. We used to make jokes about him. One guy would say, "Hell, if we could win a war with Japan by having the most spick and span base, we'd win in a walk!"

Then we got a new squadron commander. His name was Major Roger M. Remy. He was all that an officer should be. Remy wanted things to look great, but not at the expense of military efficiency. He realized our job was to be ready for war, not act as landscapers.

Finally, the major had had enough. We were scheduled to go out on a flight exercise, but Remy made sure the whole squadron was working on the grounds.

Boy, did the stuff hit the fan! Our major was really read off, but there was nothing the general could do about it.

Anyway, 'ole P. P. didn't ask for as many men on police detail as before, but we still hated that duty.

Then I made PFC, which was a real rank in those days. What it meant was I would now be in charge of the work detail. I was in command of the rest of the men who would be wearing fatigues while I wore khaki. I was smart enough not to lord it over my buddies and everything went smoothly.

Well, by lunchtime that sun was really heating up a storm. My crew started to bitch like Billy be damned.

"Jim," they pleaded, "let's stow this nonsense. It's hotter than the old Harry here and we're not really doing much. Let's secure for the day."

I thought for a while and agreed with them.

"Ok, men," I said, "time to quit. Head for the hills!"

Then I took off for the beach.

Oh, hell! Wouldn't you know it? This was the day that old P. P. decided to inspect the troops. Wow, did I get my ass chewed out! I ended up getting restricted to the base for a week, but I did not lose my stripe.

Why not? Simple. Major Remy was always sympathetic when it came to our P of P details. He probably got a chuckle out of it.

Now for a word about Major Roger Remy. He was one man you could call a great officer. The officers' manual says a good leader must look out for the welfare of his men.

That was Remy all over. He got as far as a lieutenant general and in 1960 he was killed in an automobile accident. I am sure he would have ended up head of Joint Chiefs if he had not been killed.

Well, life was not all soldiering before the war, not by a long shot. There was plenty of free time.

It seems that many of the soldiers would head for that honky-tonky stuff in Honolulu, but that wasn't really my bag. Besides those lectures they were always giving us would scare me to death. You know all those diseases floating around? Our medics had a small instrument they called the umbrella. When I think how they used that instrument to clean out your privates—well, it still scares me.

But one way or another my pay kept rising. I was anxious to go out and spend some of it.

Of course, we had a great place to drink beer right there near Hickam Field. The beer they sold was the local brand called Primo Beer. You could sit there and drink as much of that rot gut brew as you wanted, but if you drank too much, you'd see snakes. So we called that beer hall "The Snake Ranch." It wasn't my favorite hangout.

Anyway, someone told me about a place called Hilo. I had some free time coming up so I decided to try Hilo to get away from all that lowlife at Honolulu. The military had set up a place to stay on the beach there. All you had to pay was thirty-five cents a day to get your sheets laundered. It was great!

While I was there, I met a Japanese girl named Rosemary. She lived nearby with her family. She had been born in Honolulu, but her parents had come from Japan. I hadn't been out of high school but a year or two. It was like being back home and dating. I kept in touch with her until December 7 of '41. I don't know what happened to Rosemary after that, but I hope everything turned out all right. Hell, she was as American as apple pie.

All right. A year or so before the attack I had bought a sec-ondhand automobile. By December of '41 I was due to go back to the States so on December 5, '41, I sold it to another airman. He gave me $350 the next day.

Now, let's go back to the fall of '39 when I arrived at Pearl Harbor. The war in Europe had just broken out. I can remember what my mother's first letter to me had said.

"Thank God, Jim," she wrote, "you're way out there in the Pacific. If we do get into the war, there'll be no fighting in the Pacific. It will all be in France. That is what happened last time."

Well, by August of '41 our general seemed to be greatly con-cerned about the possibility of sabotage. Here's a quote from a letter I sent home at the time.

"Many of the men are on antisabotage squads. They carry shotguns downtown to Waikiki and patrol a certain area. It seems funny to send airplane mechanics downtown to do the infantry's work, especially when there aren't enough men as it is to work on the planes. I think the commanding general is off his nut."

Nevertheless, the fear of possible trouble with the large Japa-nese population on the island became an obsession with our offi-cers. That was the reason so many of our planes were lined up in a row when the attack came. They figured they'd be easier to guard that way. Maybe so. But they were also easier to destroy. And those Japanese sure did a job on them!

All right. On the night of December 6 I was real tired. I figured I wouldn't go out on the town, just stay on the post and get a real good night's sleep. So, I hit the sack real early.

The next morning I woke up at about seven o'clock. I remem-ber looking out at the harbor. It was quite a sight. The weather was absolutely beautiful. Our barracks was the nearest one to the harbor and the screen nearest my bunk had the best view of Battleship Row. Everything looked quite serene to me.

It was Sunday morning, not the best day to go to the mess hall. As each man woke up, we'd exchange pleasantries. Nothing serious. Just the same old crap.

Then shortly before eight we heard a deep thud. I looked out to the harbor and saw a big block of black smoke.

"Wow," I yelled, "the Navy has a big fire over at Pearl!"

"Big deal!" one of our guys answered. "That's their problem. They've had fires before. They can handle it. It's Sunday. I'm going back to sleep."

Well, it was a hell of a lot more serious than a fire. Now, I could see all these planes flying around. A couple of our carriers were due back soon. They'd always send their planes in first.

Holy Christ, I got a good look at one of the planes. It was definitely coming in for a torpedo run. I got a clear view of a rising sun on the wings.

"How in hell did that Jap plane get in here?" I shouted.

Now everyone is alert. Just like that, we were at war with Japan. Their planes seemed to be everywhere. We're all running around as if we're in a Chinese fire drill. Some of us tried to go outside, but an old-time first sergeant is barring the way.

"Don't go out there now," he's roaring. "Do you see those tracer bullets landing on the parade ground? There are four bullets between each tracer. You'll get your ass shot off!" He was right.

So we waited until the strafing stopped. Then we went outside, but we didn't know what to do. About a hundred yards away a group of soldiers had got ahold of three water-cooled fifties. They had set the machine guns in a row. I thought this was a little stupid, but at least they were firing at the Japanese.

Next the strafers came back. And I mean they were shooting at everybody, particularly the people in automobiles. I guess they figured anyone who had a car was a big shot.

This, of course, was nonsense. I had owned a car just two days ago and I certainly was no big shot. As a matter of fact, I was walking around with $350 in my pocket. I kept thinking about that money. What would happen to it if I were killed? Then I laughed. What the hell difference would it make to me?

In the meantime, our twelve new B-17s were coming in from the States. They were a brand-new model, which meant they had a tail gun and an upper turret.

They ended up landing all over the place. I watched one come down in the middle of a golf course. Miraculously, every plane landed safely one way or another. There was only one casualty. The crew from one plane was strafed after they got out. The flight surgeon was killed.

Anyway, the Japanese fire was deadly all right, but so was ours. The American batteries were throwing up a tremendous amount of flak. I saw a perfect group of naval antiaircraft shells going after a Japanese twin-engine plane. I could see it had retractable landing gears. The only problem with the grouping was it was slightly off target. All our shells missed and many of them started landing nearby. I saw one shell coming down too close for comfort. I immediately laid down as flat as possible.

Wham! When the shell hit, it threw me up in the air. I went up and down like a yo-yo, but I wasn't hurt.

Another boom blew open the door to our stockroom. Two of us ran in past the blown-off door. We heard someone yelling, "Gas attack, gas attack!" So we took out as many gas masks as we could carry out and started passing them out to the troops. An officer saw what we were doing and put us up for Purple Hearts.

Hell, I thought the Purple Heart was given out for wounds. All we had done was pass out gas masks. So, no Purple Heart. I did get a Silver Star, but that was a long time after December 7, 1941.

Whatever, a few weeks after the attack they raised a big fuss about the indiscriminate giving out of Purple Hearts for anything other than wounded in action.

Well, the next day I looked over the damage to Hickam. My God, it was a mess! All the landscaping work we had done didn't impress the Japanese one iota. I don't know if it would have made any difference if we had spent that time soldiering or not, but as the man said about chicken soup, "It couldn't hurt."

Oh, I guess you could say the same thing about all that time we spent checking for saboteurs. It's my opinion that when you are in the Air Corps, you should be in the Air Corps, period.

So, my trip home had to be delayed for quite a while. The Japanese may have had an edge on us with their Zeros at the beginning, but it wasn't too long before we were building better planes than the Zero and a lot more of them. I ended up getting a commission and stayed in the U.S. Army Air Force Reserves after the war. I was called up for the Korean Conflict and I spent several years either on active duty or in the Reserves after that. I was finally separated permanently in 1964.

Originally, I didn't figure on spending that much time in the military, but that's the way it ended up.

Thanksgiving Dinner

◈

Many of the men who enlisted from 1935 through 1940 had mainly gone into the services because halfway decent jobs were hard to get. True, twenty-one dollars a month wasn't much but along with that went your keep and your medical bills.

And if what I was told was even partially true, the food was better than the meals one would receive in the service in 1943, particularly if one was in a small detachment somewhere.

When a holiday came along, the chow was really good. The following is the Thanksgiving Day dinner as served to the troops at Hickam Field two weeks before the attack. It was the last great feast for several of these men.

Thanksgiving Day Dinner
Hickam Field, T.H.

Assorted Fruit Cocktail
Turkey Broth with Rice
Hearts of Celery   Ripe and Green Olives   Sweet Gherkins
Roast Tom Turkey, stuffed with Chestnuts
Giblet Gravy
Baked Southern Ham, Champagne Sauce
Dixie Candied Yams   Cream Whipped Potatoes
Green Fresh Peas
Head Lettuce with Asparagus Tips
Thousand Island Dressing
Parker House Rolls   Fruit Cake
Mince Pie, Hard Sauce   Pumpkin Pie
Cherry Pie a la Mode
Roquefort Cheese   Hard Crackers
Fresh Lemonade   Coffee
Fruits   Nuts   Bon Bons
Cigars   Cigarettes

Officers, I Hate Officers

◆

In 1941 there was not only a military separation between officers and enlisted men but there was a very rigid social separation also.

One of the men I talked to was named Bill Peterson. Bill was from San Francisco. On the day he landed at Pearl, he tried to get a ride to the Schofield Barracks. Bill, a corporal in the U.S. Army, was about to transfer into the 25th Division.

He finally located a ride in a jeep, driven by a second lieutenant. It turned out the officer was also from San Francisco. The trip took half an hour or so. They spent it talking about their hometown.

They arrived at Schofield. The officer turned the jeep in and they started to walk down the company street, side by side.

All of a sudden the officer gave Peterson a very stern look.

"Corporal," he said, "you'd better walk behind me."

All right, here it is fifty years later and Peterson still remembered that story. After he told it to me, he just shook his head and very sarcastically muttered, "Shit!"

I think James Jones brings out this division between the men and the officers very well in his classic novel *From Here to Eternity*.

One of the main figures in the book is Top Sergeant Warden. Most enlisted men will tell you it's the top kick who really runs a company.

Well, Warden is having a steaming affair with his company commander's wife. He is really playing with dynamite.

100

Anyway, the sergeant's girlfriend is trying to have Warden get a commission. Then she can ditch her husband and marry her lover. When she tells Warden, he is hardly overjoyed.

"There is a way," she says. "I've been thinking about it. You've got to become an officer. Dana will be glad to help you. As your commanding officer it will be a feather in his cap if his top soldier becomes a second lieutenant. Then you will be sent back to the States."

"What," says Warden, "me become an officer?"

"Yes, then I'll leave Dana and we can be married back in the States."

"But I hate officers! I've always hated officers and I always will hate officers."

And that's the way it was on the island of Oahu in December of 1941.

The Four Marines of Kaneohe Bay

Eddie K. Misonie
Walter Kozoil
Wesley Boot
John Kowalik

◈

"Single men in barracks don't grow into plaster saints."

—From the poem "Tommy"
by Rudyard Kipling.

There were ninety-three U.S. Marines stationed at the Kaneohe Bay Naval Station on the island of Oahu. This naval station was on the Pacific Ocean, northeast of Pearl Harbor. It offered an ideal entrance for planes on their way to bomb the American fleet.

While Pearl Harbor was the number-one target of the Japanese, it was also immensely important to destroy as many of the American planes on the ground as possible.

And this is why the first hostile planes appeared over Kaneohe on the seventh of December 1941.

With the help of Walter Kozoil, I had the good fortune to interview four of these former Marines at the American Airlines Admirals Club at Chicago's O'Hare Airport. I just let the tape run.

There is a dash to denote a new speaker.

—You know the old Marine Corps adage, "Good duty is your

previous post and your next station." It never is where you are currently stationed.

—"That's right and let me tell you, at Kaneohe we did have good duty, but we were always bitching when we were stationed there.

—Shit, did you ever hear about a Marine unit that didn't bitch?

—No, and you never will. But there were only ninety-three Marines at the air station and we lived high on the hog. The chow was great. We had a pool table, a Ping-Pong table, all the luxuries of home.

—Yeah, and very little chicken shit. Our CEO, Major Donahue, was aces, one of the great old Marine officers like Devereux, Carlson, and Puller. Like those men.

—I'll tell you one thing that wasn't so hot, that was when the eagle shit.

—Oh, boy. $10.50 if you were a buck ass private and a little more if you were a PFC.

—Wow and could that dough go fast! There was always a big crap game going on in the head on payday. You could drop a couple of bucks there. Then you might take the bus into Honolulu. You knew you could go get a roll in the hay for two or three bucks at any number of cathouses.

—Next, you had a great selection of any number of slop chutes. By the time you'd get back to the base you had very little dough left to tide you over for two weeks.

—Don't forget the Bull Durham. It seems to me that just about everyone would roll their own. For fifty cents you would get enough tobacco to last for days.

—Yeah, as long as you looked out for the leeches. There was always a guy who would send money home every two weeks and then spend the next week or two bumming a smoke from the rest of us.

—You can say that again. I had a word for those clowns. "Semper Fi, Mac," I would say, then give 'em the finger.

—OK, you mentioned the cathouses. Do you remember that

guy Birlschit? He used to say that he was so long that the girls would give 'im a free one.

—Yeah, haw, haw, I always called him bird shit. Do you remember the time he had the crabs?

—I'll say. The poor guy, not only did he have them on his balls, but under his arms and in his eyebrows.

—That's right. We wouldn't let him sleep in the guards' quarters. He was so lousy we threw him out.

—Yeah, but he could come back in to use the head. Remember that special throne marked "crabs"?

—Haw, haw. That's right. Tripod, that was the nickname he liked, was the only person I ever saw sitting on it.

They also had a throne marked "VD." Those two signs were in heads all over the Corps.

—But not in the officers' heads. Perish the thought.

—Of course not. Marine officers never caught the clap or the crabs. Haw, haw.

—Maybe not, but I had a special girl named Gypsy. She worked at the New Senator Hotel. She would tell me what a great lover I was and that I should come back when the fleet was out to sea so we could have a little time to talk.

—Oh, for Christ's sake. I remember Gypsy. She used to tell everyone to come back. When she wasn't busy. That was good for business.

—Oh, no, not my Gypsy. She had the hots for me. I'd like to see her today.

—Hell, you idiot, she's probably well over seventy by now. When we go back to Pearl next year, you should ask for her at the New Senator Hotel, if it's still there that is.

—Yeah, also ask if they have a special rate for senior citizens, but make sure you don't have a heart attack.

—Right on. And my question is, are you sure you can remember what to do?

—Speak for yourself. But, you remember when, shortly after the attack, the madams tried to raise the going rate from three bucks to five and the Honolulu *Star Citizen* had the special editorial saying they shouldn't do that to our boys in uniform?

—I sure do. And I heard some big-shot generals and admirals told the madams they'd better not try it or the whole Hotel Street area would be declared off-limits. That did it. The rate stayed at three.

—I remember that well. And do you guys remember this? I've been carrying it around for fifty years.

—Oh, Christ, that's a rain check. If you were too drunk to perform, they'd give you that and tell you to come back when you were sober. They ran those places like an automotive assembly line. They wanted to get you in and out in a hurry.

—Did they ever. But remember, we were shut out from any good-looking, so-called nice girls. They were officers' stuff.

—Well, you want to hear about the attack. OK, the four of us were part of the Marine detachment at the Naval Air Station, Kaneohe Bay, Territory of Hawaii. We had joined the Corps in 1940 and '41. Many of the other Marines had been in for years. A few had served time in Nicaragua or China.

—I believe the Naval Air Station was opened in '39. Our detachment ended up with ninety-three Marines. And those of us who survived the war have tried to have an annual gathering each year.

—And when I arrived they were still working on the base. The people doing the work mainly lived near. We got to know many of them and their families. They'd have us over for dinner frequently. They lived in grass shacks and houses of corrugated steel.

—The people in Honolulu were a different story. It seems to me that most of the people living there looked down on enlisted men. Not all of them, of course, but most.

—We were located almost directly across the island from Pearl Harbor. When we'd get liberty, a truck would take us to Kailua. There we'd catch a bus to Honolulu. You'd have to be back at Kailua by midnight to catch the truck back to the air station. I guess they figured that everything we wanted would be on Hotel Street.

—OK. On Saturday night, December 6, none of the four of us left the base. We had horses at the station and we had a big luau over at the stables. Plenty of booze and food. I think we had a pig roast.

—So, the next morning, I think it was about 7:30, we were all sitting around and beating our gums about something. I know I had a bit of a hangover (the other three laughed and nodded their heads), when I heard some airplane engines coming over. I don't know who first realized they were Japs, but Johnny Kowalik here was the first American to fire at them. He grabbed a bolt-action Springfield rifle and ran out and fired a clip at the enemy.

—But I didn't have much of a chance of hitting one. It just annoyed the hell out of me that the Japs could do to us what they were doing and not even be shot at.

—And the first casualty of the attack was also in our lash-up. His name was Tony DeJacimo. He was nailed by a Japanese bullet the same time that Kowalik was firing his rifle at the Nips. Tony is also from Chicago and would be here today only he has just had open heart surgery.

Anyway, you look on the map and you'll see that Kaneohe was the first logical target for the Japs to hit if they wanted to destroy our aircraft.

—Well, their number-one target was our carriers. But they wanted to also knock out as much of our air power as possible. Remember the Japanese fleet was only a few hundred miles away. They sure as hell didn't want any of our planes bombing their carriers.

—The amazing thing to me, though, is that someone at Kaneohe actually called Pearl Harbor and told them that we were under attack.

—Yeah, that's right, and the man he talked to at Pearl told him to go to hell. Wouldn't believe him. Can you fathom that?

Our biggest problem was our weapons. We just weren't ready.

We had received some BARs and a machine gun, but they were still in the Cosmoline. We did fire our rifles at the Nips, but the three or four planes that were shot down were hit by the sailors. They had several machine guns going at the Japs. They also took most of the Jap fire. Of our eighteen men killed, they were all in the U.S. Navy.

—Oh, I can't overestimate the shock of the whole thing. Our Major Donehoo who lived a mile or so from the base jumped into his car the minute he heard the first shot. By the time he got to the barracks, he had God knows how many bullet holes in his car. I mean it was just riddled, but he didn't have a scratch.

—That's right. He didn't. He took cover with the rest of us. Then he grabbed me.

"Go out and change my rear left tire," he said. "They've shot it full of holes."

"Christ, Major," I said, "you can't go anywhere in that car. It's a wreck. Besides, I don't want to get killed changing a tire."

The major thought awhile, then he laughed.

"Oh, hell," he chuckled. "I don't want you getting killed over a goddamn tire. Forget it." That was the major.

—In spades. But I'll tell you one thing I've never been able to figure out. Why didn't they set our oil tanks on fire? We had thousands of gallons of oil. They could have set a blaze that would take weeks to put out.

—I agree. And so, as I understand it, they just didn't seem to want to go after the oil tanks anywhere. Hell, they could have set the whole island of Oahu afire.

—They must have known where all the oil was. They only knocked out one of our hangars, the one where we kept all our spare parts. They knew what hangar to hit.

—But, think back. We all felt they were going to follow up with an invasion. They would have wanted to capture that oil. Makes sense to me anyhow.

—You're on target there. Most of us felt the bombing had just been to soften us up for an invasion. By nightfall we'd taken our

BARs and machine guns out of the Cosmoline. We were lined up on one side of the field and the Navy was lined up on the other.

—That's right and you know the only thing I can remember about that night was the rain. We hadn't had anything to eat. We were starved. I could have eaten the bark off a tree. Then they gave us some scrambled eggs.

Hell, they were swimming in rainwater.

—Haw, haw. That's right, I don't recommend wet scrambled eggs no matter how hungry you are. Those eggs beat Spam, but that's just about all.

—What I remember about that night was the scuttlebutt. Every five minutes we'd get the word that the Japs had landed in a different place.

—And how about the parachute drops. The Japs were supposed to have jumped throughout the islands. At dawn the Nips were expected to land a hundred thousand men to capture Oahu.

—Hundred thousand? Hell, they could have taken the place with thirty thousand.

—Of course, we just didn't stop to think how vulnerable those Jap carriers would be if they sat off Pearl too long. Remember, none of our carriers had been at anchor the morning of the seventh.

—You're right. But we sure as hell thought they were coming after the two waves of bombers had gone over.

—God knows how many shots were fired that night. I remember someone spotted a small boat adrift in the bay. The boys fired countless shots into that tub, finally sinking it. My, oh, my, what a victory!

—Well, as you know, the invasion never came off. Our group was eventually broken up and we all went our merry way. By the battle of Okinawa, we'd all been shipped back to the States and were out in the Pacific for the second time. Then came the big bomb and it was all over. Japan was on her knees, but she surely didn't stay there long.

—Several years went by, then someone had the brilliant idea that those Marines who were at Kaneohe during the Japanese attack should get together for a reunion. And we've been doing it ever since.

Hotel Street

While working on previous books on veterans the subject of "scarlet ladies" has always come up. The 1918 doughboys had their Bar Le Duc. Many of the World War II Marines spoke fondly of a place on New Caledonia called the Pink House. The Korean War veteran's dream was an R&R trip to Japan, but most of them did not get one until they were on their way home.

For the American serviceman on the island of Oahu in December of '41 there was something called Hotel Street. It was in a class by itself. The subject came up in all seventy interviews I conducted all over the U.S. Soldiers, sailors, Marines, they all mentioned Hotel Street.

Bill Anderson told me you had all kinds of stores on the first floor. But on the top floor, or floors, there was always a bordello. It was three dollars for three minutes. You would go into a small room and undress. Next you went into another small room. Your lovely would be lying in bed, waiting for you. As most of the customers were twenty or so years of age, your visit would be short. There'd be another small room to get dressed in. Things had to move fast at all times.

There was always a lineup of men, waiting their turn. One former sailor told me the line on Saturday night could be two blocks long. As he told me this, he was quickly corrected by another veteran.

"Baloney, you mean two *miles* long, don't you?"

Be that as it may, there was always a line going into the wee hours of the morning, especially on Saturday night.

In *From Here to Eternity* Private Pruitt's girlfriend worked at a place called the New Congress Club. Strangely enough, the New Senators Hotel was probably the most liked whorehouse on the island. But, as I was told, like all the others, the call was "Keep the line moving!" This was up to the madam. If she spotted a patron perhaps a little too far gone to perform, she would pull him out of line. If he had already paid, he would be given a rain check. It would be signed by one of the girls. The patron could then return when sober and be given his pound of flesh. One of the men showed me a card from the Congress Club. It was signed by a girl named Ruby.

Now, if anyone is interested in researching this further, I wholeheartedly suggest your reading *The Revolt of Mamie Stover* by Bill Huies. It explains the then number-one attraction on Oahu in detail.

Now, the spring of 1991, I was attending a meeting of the San Berdu chapter of the Pearl Harbor Survivors Association.

Just as the meeting was about to break up a very dignified gentleman stood up. "Ladies and gentlemen," he said, "I'd like to propose a toast to 'Leaping Linda,' the best young lady of the New Senators Hotel in 1941."

He was greeted by a good deal of cheers and laughter. But I noticed several of the men had raised their glasses. They all had a sad, contemplative look in their eyes as if they were looking back over half a century.

James Bowling

◈

Gee, Henry, Pearl Harbor was a long time ago. I was fifteen years of age, living in Paducah, Kentucky. That's the town Irving S. Cobb made famous. I can remember him well. He died when I was in the Army in '44. But I've got just about every book he ever wrote.

Well, on December 7 I'd gone to church and Sunday school. Even sang in the choir. You did things like that in Paducah fifty years ago.

After that a crew of us started playing sandlot football. We were all on the Paducah High School squad and had been told not to play sandlot ball, but we played it anyway.

All of a sudden this kid came riding by on his bicycle.

"The Japs have bombed Pearl Harbor; you'd better get to a radio."

My God, we were stunned. I mean we were absolutely stunned. One of our group spoke up. "I don't know if you guys know where Pearl Harbor is, but I sure do. My big brother is out there."

What could we say? It did bring the whole thing closer to us. Here we were, standing in a lot on Paducah and Broadway in western Kentucky and the brother of one of my friends is fighting for his life way out in the Pacific. Hell, we all knew our pal's brother. He'd been playing football with us just a few years back. Well, we all hopped on our bikes and headed for home.

When I arrived, I shouted for somebody to turn on the radio.

My family, and I believe most of Paducah, were internationalists. My dad had been complaining about the dictators ever since Mussolini had invaded Ethiopia. Dad had been in the Army in World War I and was always fearful about another world war. He knew it was coming.

"Now we are in," Dad said. "Good, I hope Germany and Italy jump in with Japan. Let's really teach them a lesson this time."

Anyway, no other part of the country backed the President in the war that had just started any more than western Kentucky. I think that just about every one of those lads I was playing football with on December 7 enlisted as quickly as they could.

John Grand Pre, Fireman 1st Class, U.S.S. *Oklahoma*

◆

"Man's love for women may wane from day to day, but that
for his brother is eternal."   —The Koran

There is one thing I'd like to straighten out. People ask me if we
were all ashore, dead drunk, or just screwing off when the attack
came. That's all baloney; a great big fallacy.

In the first place, you almost never had an overnight liberty
unless you were married. And most of us were single on December
7, 1941. We had to be back aboard by 0100.

Of course, this didn't include the commissioned officers. Many
of them had their wives at Pearl, or said they did, but as I remember it, most of them were also aboard when the attack came. We
were there all right when the Japanese came. It's just that it happened so fast there was nothing we could do about it.

Look at it this way. In '41 many families had their big meal of
the week between twelve and one P.M. on Sunday. Let's say your
family had just sat down for this meal. Dad is about to serve the
main course when a group of these clowns burst in with tommy
guns and open up on your gathering. That's the way it was.

All right, back to 1940. I was living on the family farm in
North Dakota. I had never seen a sailor in uniform much less the
Pacific Ocean. I was a genuine midwestern landlubber. Everything
I knew about the Navy came from those Dick Powell or Fred
Astaire movies. You know, "Shipmates stand together," "Don't
give up the ship," and all that stuff.

114

Well, in July of '40 my older brother Arthur joined the U.S. Navy. He kept writing home and telling us how great Navy life was. I had just graduated from high school and was looking around for a job. I found nothing. Remember, Old Man Depression was still very much alive in North Dakota.

So, I decided to join the Navy also. The idea of twenty-one dollars a month and all my clothing, food, and medical care was very appealing. They did not have any of the so-called kiddie cruises then. They came later. I signed up for six years. Little did I realize it would end up being a twenty-six-year career.

First they sent me to Omaha where I was sworn in and from there it was boot camp in San Diego. When that was over, they asked me where I wanted to go. At that time, the Navy seemed to encourage brothers serving together, so I asked them to ship me to the U.S.S. *Oklahoma* at Pearl Harbor. The *Okie*, or *Okie Marv* as it was frequently called by the crew, was a battleship in the Pacific Fleet. They quickly put me on another battlewagon, the U.S.S. *Tennessee* and I was off for Honolulu where I joined the crew of the *Oklahoma*.

I was put in the black gang [working in the boiler room] alongside of brother Arthur. This was definitely the peacetime Navy. I soon was in love with it.

I did have one serious complaint. When on liberty, the men over twenty-one would get together and drink beer at the local bars. I had to miss out on these gatherings.

You see, I was only eighteen years of age. This meant that I couldn't go to any of the bars. You had to have an ID card proving that you were twenty-one.

And there was no fooling around. They were tougher than a cobb about it. No proof and they'd send you out.

This was something that I used to laugh at. Here I was, supposed to be protecting these people and I couldn't even buy a beer. I've ofttimes wondered how many of my shipmates who were killed on December 7 were in the same boat.

As a matter of fact, most of the merchants in Honolulu didn't seem to be happy when the enlisted sailors came into their stores. The town just wasn't big enough for the fleet.

Oh, it wasn't as bad as Norfolk, Virginia, where they had signs that said, "No sailors or dogs allowed," but it was pretty bad.

There was an exception. This was a honky-tonk area called Hotel Street. You'd be welcome there at any hour of the day.

But, oh, my God, it was unbelievable. That Hotel Street was just one big whorehouse. I stayed in the Navy for almost thirty years and I saw hundreds of ports like Tsingta, China, where they had the famous, or infamous, "House of a Thousand Assholes," but I never again saw a place like Hotel Street in Honolulu.

The men would be in line around the block. There is nothing that will make young men miss a woman any more than a month or so out at sea, living in close proximity with other men. And you could always tell which sailors had enjoyed the services of the ladies of Hotel Street.

The Navy didn't give a damn where you went on liberty, but they didn't want you bringing back any VD to your ship.

So, most of the sailors who had partaken of Venus's charms would stop at a pro station and get this little tube of goo. You were to stick the tube into the entrance of your penis and squeeze. Then you'd rub the goo into your pubic hair. It was also supposed to kill the crabs.

Well, it was almost impossible not to stain your whites. When we'd spot a sailor coming on board with a stain on his crotch, we'd yell, "Hotel Street, Hotel Street."

All right, let's get to the big day. The *Okie* sailed into Pearl Friday morning, December 5. I just made fireman 1st class and was feeling real salty. When you are a young kid in the Navy, being salty is a big thing. You know, "I've sailed by more lighthouses than you've walked around corners." Things like that.

Anyway, we were set to have a real big admiral's inspection Monday morning. After we tied up at Berth F-5, outboard of the *Maryland*, we really turned to, opening voids, copperdowns, everything there was to open. That's the reason we capsized eight minutes or so after we took that first torpedo. I don't think we got a single shot off at the Japanese.

So, Sunday morning was the one time in the old peacetime Navy when everything was relaxed. If you did not go to church, you could sleep in.

A bunch of us had drawn our chow and had come back to our sacks. On the *Okie* we had these tables in a rack where we slept. We'd pull out the tables, eat our food, then return the tables to their rack.

We'd done this and were sitting around in our skivvies, shooting the shit, when we first heard all this noise. One of our guys was positively pissed off, "What in the hell are those bastards doing," he roared, "having maneuvers on Sunday morning?"

So, we figured, what the hell, we'd better meander down to our battle stations. That's what we were doing when a shipmate stuck his head down the hatch.

"Holy shit," he bellowed, "this is the real thing, those fuckin' Japs are bombing us." Shortly after this, we took our first fish, then another.

Oh, you wouldn't believe the confusion. We were halfway down to our stations when our beautiful ship started to capsize.

Now we really didn't know what to do. They sounded "abandon ship," but how in hell could we do this? We knew we were going to fill up with water. It looked like we were trapped. This CPO above decks was yelling, "Get the hell off, get your ass off." I didn't know how I was going to do this, but I found out in a hurry. Here's what I did.

There was a big guy, a chief water tender, by the name of Day, in the engineers' washroom. His name was Francis Day. He could look down on us. He yelled to me.

"Grand Pre, Grand Pre, get your ass up here on the double."

So I climbed up the ladder as quickly as I could.

"John, you're going out that porthole," he told me.

Hell, I only weighed about 130 pounds then, but I didn't think I could make it.

"How in God's name can I do that?" I yelled.

"Damn it, I'm going to shove you through."

Poor Day. He weighed in at about 240. He knew he couldn't get out, but he was going to get as many of us as possible off that capsized ship.

Now, you have no idea how you can wiggle your body when you have to, particularly when a man like Day is pushing you. With his help I got through. I slid down the side of the ship into the water.

There was another big man, a chaplain named Father Schmidt, over in A Division's washroom. He was doing the same thing, even though he was also personally doomed. I don't know how many lives these two men saved, but it must have been a lot. I think they both were awarded the Congressional Medal of Honor. Father Schmidt has some kind of memorial in his home state of Iowa. In my book these two were real heroes.

Well, there I was in the water. I was trying to swim, but the water was fast filling with oil.

Fortunately, a launch from the *Maryland* was cruising around looking for survivors. They picked me up. They were trying to wipe the oil from my eyes when the second Japanese wave came over. The capsized *Okie* was helpless, but the *Maryland* had all her guns blazing. I think the *Maryland* took just one hit, a bomb aft, and they stayed in the fight till the end.

After the second wave had left the area, a stunned island of Oahu licked her wounds. I started looking for my brother Arthur. Every time I'd see anyone from my division, I'd ask if he'd seen my brother. It got so I'd be asking the same guy I'd asked a half hour before. Finally, one guy nodded in approval.

"Jeez, Arthur," he roared, "he was around here a little while ago, asking for you."

You see, we looked a lot alike, but at least he made me feel good.

But just for a day or so, then I got the tragic news. My brother did get off the ship, but when he was swimming, a Japanese pilot riddled him with lead. My beloved brother was gone.

To make matters worse, the government fouled up. They sent a telegram back home telling my parents that both their sons had been killed. It wasn't until the end of the month that my mother received a telegram telling her I was alive. But the damage had been done; Mother died in the next year.

I stayed in the Navy until the war was over, then shipped over for another cruise. I didn't leave the service till 1963. I did lose another ship before World War II was over, when the *Northampton* went down off Guadalcanal.

Well, this all happened a long time ago, but I have never stopped missing Arthur. Every time I hear people moaning about what a horrible thing we did at Hiroshima, I think of the sucker punch the Japanese pulled on us on December 7, 1941. Then I think of my brother, Arthur, and I shed no tears for the Japanese dead.

Maybe We Were Lucky at Pearl—
Ensign Warren Flynn,
U.S.S. *Maryland*

◈

I was at Dartmouth College when Hitler went into Czechoslovakia. I remember a group of us sitting around hearing the news on the radio. One of us spoke up.

"Hell, gentlemen," he said, "that's thousands of miles from here. They can take care of that idiot over there." The rest is history.

So, in 1939 I heard about a program where I could get a Reserve commission in the Navy. It was no snap, believe me, but I got it. Several months after I got my commission, Roosevelt called up the Reserves.

In October I was sent to the U.S.S. *Maryland* at Pearl Harbor. The *Maryland* was out to sea so they stuck me aboard the *Oklahoma*. That was in dry dock. I was to join the *Maryland* when she returned to Pearl.

By this time I was a lieutenant junior grade. I was an engineering officer, which meant my duty station was way down below. My chances of getting strafed were nil, but if a bomb got down near my station, I would have been blown to kingdom come.

For instance, if I had still been on the *Oklahoma* when the attack came, I would have been a goner.

Now, let me say a few things about our enlisted crew. I know many of them had gone into the Navy due to the Depression to learn a trade.

120

Well, they sure learned it. Things were always going wrong with our engines. Those machinist's mates could do wonders and in a hurry.

Anyway, I had appraised the situation thoroughly and I was convinced that war with Japan was just around the corner. Who knows? Maybe our next patrol would be for all the marbles.

But as far as the Japanese coming all the way to Pearl, I never gave it a thought.

Nevertheless, come they did! Whatever, when you see a movie on Pearl, a panicking sailor is loudly yelling, "General Quarters, General Quarters, this is no drill!"

Well, that's not exactly the way I remember it. It seems to me this sailor was yelling, "General Quarters, General Quarters—this is NO SHIT! The Japs are here!" I guess that salty language doesn't quite fit in the history books. But it surely got through to the men on the ships. I stayed down below the whole morning, fearing a torpedo attack or a bomb getting through, but neither happened.

I finally got a chance to get topside around noon. I'm sure other sailors have told you of the shock they got looking out at the Harbor.

Now, here's a funny one. They had closed the bars ashore after the attack started and kept them closed for a week or so. I had a close pal who was out to sea. I called his wife to see if she had heard from him. He was on a tin can. She hadn't. But she had a great suggestion.

She asked me to meet her at a restaurant. I did and she showed up with a bottle of top bourbon. We drowned our sorrows together, then I returned to the *Maryland*.

And by the way, her husband did come back in. He survived the war and when I last heard, they were still married.

All right, you asked me what did I think of the Pearl Harbor attack. Well, it was a Greek tragedy. We lost twenty-six hundred or so people, but all the Japanese got out of it was two battleships sunk and a few other minor ships destroyed.

Oh, they finished off a hundred or so of our planes, but most of them were obsolete anyway.

People make a lot out of all the chances we had to be warned, but we were still caught with our pants down.

All right. What if we had been warned a day or so ahead of time? The battleships would have been taken out to sea in different directions. You know what happened to the H.M.S. *Prince of Wales* and the H.M.S. *Repulse* a few days later without air coverage. They were lost with just about all hands.

You see, if four or even all eight of the battlewagons had faced those two or three hundred Jap planes out at sea, it would have been a massacre.

As for the attacking Japanese, they should have bombed the hell out of the Navy yard, not the battleships. That would have really hurt us badly.

No, I don't think anyone got a great victory out of Pearl Harbor. The one thing it did accomplish was it showed once and for all that the day of the aircraft carrier was upon us. The battleship's day had come and gone.

Joseph St. Pierre, Gunner's Mate,
U.S.S. *Phoenix*

◈

Actually, I was born in Canada, but my father took our family to the States when I was a youngster.

As I grew older I became more and more interested in joining the military. Someone told me I should look into the Connecticut National Guard. So I went to see the guy who did the recruiting. He looked me over.

"How old are you, young man?"

"Sixteen."

"Come back next week when you are eighteen." I've always thought that was quite colorful, but I never did come back.

I ended up joining the C.C.C. They sent me to Maine where I spent a year or two. I eventually came back to Hartford, but there still wasn't much to do. I'd always wanted to be a cook so I went to work for the man who ran the West Hartford Diner. The center where the diner was located was quite small in those days, but you should see it now.

All right, I was more or less marking time at the diner, trying to figure out what to do with my life. They hired a new waiter just out of the Navy. He gave me the word.

"Jeez, Joe," he said, "go into the Navy for a cruise. You'll love it."

That sounded pretty good to me. Besides, I figured I could get a good start as a cook in the Navy.

So, I joined up, but I never did get to be a cook. First they sent me to Newport, Rhode Island, for boot camp. They had this sailor quizzing us.

"St. Pierre," he asked, "what do you want to do in the Navy?"

"Be a cook," I answered.

"That's fine," he said.

That was it. Or was it? I ended up on the U.S.S. *Phoenix* that was commissioned at the Philadelphia Navy Yard in 1938. I am what you call a plank owner. We soon shoved off for Pearl Harbor.

For the next two to three years we went in and out of that beautiful harbor. When we'd come back to Pearl, we'd get some time off, depending on how long we'd been out in the Pacific.

In those days we'd rarely wear our uniforms ashore. I rented a locker where I stowed my civilian clothes. I used to play a lot of golf. I kept my clubs and a good camera there. The place I'd play golf was the Royal Hawaiian. It was owned by the hotel and was a hell of a fine course.

Another thing I enjoyed was rifle shooting. Most of the ships had rifle teams. I was on ours and was a pretty fair shot, if I do say so myself. There was a good deal of competition among the ships, not only in rifle shooting but in baseball, football, basketball, just about every sport you can name. It was all part of the peacetime Navy.

Back to that cook's school business. It never happened, not for me anyway. I ended up a gunner's mate. Maybe if I'd asked to be a gunner's mate, they would have made me a cook.

Anyway, one time we'd been out for a very long cruise and when we got back in, some of the old hands were given five days off. Four of us got together and decided we'd walk around Oahu. One of our group was named Winchell. We'd either call him Walter or "All the Ships at Sea." You know, after the columnist.

So, we started out. Our only problem was we'd run into bars along the way. You'd think we were out to drink the island dry. We got stuck in one place and we stayed there till we got sober.

Now, don't think we were all drunks. We weren't. But when

you're out to sea for a month or two, you can work up a powerful thirst. Hell, when I was working at the West Hartford Diner, we'd see a bunch of kids come in on a Saturday night three sheets to the wind. Most of us weren't much older than those kids. We liked to blow off steam every now and then just like they did.

Whatever, we had only five days leave. We had already used up four. We would have to really hustle if we were going to be back on time. We were halfway around the island so it didn't make any difference which way we went.

We had no sooner started than a young lady showed up in a sports car with the top down.

"Where are you fellows going?" she asked.

"Back to the *Phoenix* at Pearl Harbor."

"This is your lucky day. That is the way I am going. Hop in."

So, we all squeezed in. It was a little close, but nobody seemed to mind.

Hell, it turned out she was a pro from Hotel Street. It was her time of the month so a kindly madam had given her two days off and a car so she could see the island. They can say what they want about those girls, but she was aces with us.

Now, do you want to hear something funny? Sometime in early November we took the *Phoenix* to the Philippines on a goodwill cruise. We went to Cebu, Manila, all over the place.

On our way back we ran into a problem. All of a sudden they sounded a surprise General Quarters. We ran to our battle stations. We rammed the bloody ammunition up the spout. We were all standing by wondering what was happening. Our officers were edgy as hell. I always figured something was out there, but our officers didn't know any more than we did.

Then came the secure from General Quarters order. All we were told was we had been near a concentration of strange ships. They had to be Japanese. If we had fired on them, the whole history of the world might have been changed. We would probably have been sunk, but there would not have been a complete disaster at Pearl.

All right. On Saturday, December 6, one of my buddies went ashore and staked out our claims at Waikiki for Sunday. What you'd do was stick an umbrella in the sand and that area was yours. I planned to spend Sunday on the beach.

Well, I was in charge of the Geedunk stand. Another sailor was called the Captain of the Head. We used to trade favors with each other. I could usually shower alone and sit on the trough by myself.

So, on the morning of the seventh I was showering when my friend stuck his head into the shower.

"Hey, Joe, you'd better get your ass on the ball. The Japanese are bombing us. This means war!"

"You're kidding."

"I am like hell! We're at war. I can see the Jap planes. They're going after the battlewagons."

So, I put on my short pants and went topside. A bosun's mate spotted me.

"Hey, Joe, you can work that crane. Help me get some of this crap out of here. We've got to start firing as soon as possible." So I helped the bosun; then I went to my five-incher, gun number two.

If anything, our gun crews were overtrained. We'd been doing this for years without an enemy to fire at. Now it was the real thing.

As a light cruiser we didn't have any 20- or 40-millimeter antiaircraft guns. We had the five-inchers and several .50 caliber machine guns. By the time the second wave of Japanese planes came over, we were ready for them. I'm quite sure I did hit a Betty, one of the slower Japanese planes. Others might have hit it also, but I know I did. All right, if you look over at Ford Island from the Navy yard, the *Phoenix* was at anchor to the right of Ford where Battleship Row was located. It was the battleships the Japanese were after. Seeing there were no carriers at Pearl, they wanted to sink our battleships.

And you know how the Japanese are. When they're given a

target, they'll give their life if need be to get that target. But if for one reason or another they can't hit the target, that's it. They're not apt to look for an alternate target.

Well, the *Phoenix* was not on their list. I can't tell you how many times they flew over our ship, but we weren't touched. The battleships, yes. They went after every one of them. Even the *Utah*, which really wasn't a battleship any longer, but not the *Phoenix*. We did find a spent Japanese slug aboard our ship. I think one of our guys kept it for a souvenir.

I'll tell you another thing that I later found out. Our log stated that we had seen several large Japanese bombing planes that had U.S. marks on their wings.

Well, the joke's on us. They weren't Japanese. Twelve U.S. B-17s arrived at Pearl from the States just as the first wave was ending. Some genius back in Washington wouldn't let them carry bombs or machine-gun ammunition.

Who knows? If they had had bombs aboard, perhaps they could have found the Japanese carriers. If they had sunk one or two carriers, it could have meant all the difference in the world.

Well, that's one foul-up. But for the rest of my days I will wonder what those ships were we had detected a few days before Pearl Harbor. We never did see them, but they were there.

So, after the attack, we went patrolling for a week or so. We found nothing. Then we returned to Pearl. I got a chance to go ashore.

Wow! What a shock I got! I went to my locker. That son of a bitch who ran those lockers had emptied them all out and disappeared. My golf clubs, camera, civilian clothing, even my riding stick, were gone forever.

So be it. We next took off for San Francisco with a cargo of civilians. I checked but that bird who'd cleaned out my locker was not aboard.

Anyway, when we reached San Francisco, there was no liberty time. We all turned to loading our ship with provisions for Pearl. We quickly turned around and headed back to Honolulu.

We no sooner arrived than we loaded up again with civilians and headed back to San Francisco.

This time we did go ashore and it was great. Once the American people realized we had been at Pearl they couldn't do enough for us.

I spent the rest of the war on the *Phoenix*. When it was over, I ended up in Australia. I met my future wife, got married, and stayed there for several years.

Well, it's half a century since the Japanese surprised us all at Pearl Harbor. But every now and again I can remember when we were near what must have been Japanese ships around the first of December in '41. What if we had started World War II then and there? History sure would have been changed.

Why Didn't They Bomb Our Oil Supply?

OK. My name is Ken Creese. I was born and raised in San Diego, graduated from Herbert Hoover High School, and do you know who was a few years ahead of me?

(Author—Yes, Ted Williams.)

That's right. I doubt if he even knew who I was. He used to be a pitcher in those days. A big, tall, skinny kid but could he whip that bat! A bunch of us used to go to all the games. Ted was a good high school pitcher, but it was his hitting that stood out.

After high school he signed with the San Diego Padres in the Pacific Coast League. I saw him play several games there, but I never did see him in the major leagues. He retired just before we had an American League team out here.

Well, I went into the Navy in the summer of '41. I was just seventeen at the time. When I got to Pearl Harbor, I was assigned to the U.S.S. *Detroit*. It was a four-stack light cruiser. I was still seventeen when the Japanese attacked us. My ambition is to be the last surviving member of the Pearl Harbor Survivors Association. We'll see.

So, the *Detroit* had been out on patrol. We came back in on Friday the fifth of December. The fleet was going to have a big inspection on Monday, the eighth. The large majority of the ships had everything open. That's why the *Oklahoma* went over so fast.

Anyway, the *Detroit* was lucky. A torpedo just missed us and was buried in the mud. We retrieved it the next day and that's how we found out the Japanese had special torpedoes made for the shallow water at Pearl.

After the second wave of their planes had come and gone, we started to steam up for sea. There was a rumor that the Japanese were landing troops on the other side of Oahu. We went out to see if this was true. It wasn't.

Well, we ended up being one of the few ships to leave the harbor within twenty-four hours or so of the bombing. I know the *St. Louis* was with us and I think the *Chicago* and the *Omaha* were also there. We found nothing.

But, you know, one of the biggest mistakes they made was in not hitting our fuel and oil reserves. Hell, with all the oil and gas we had, they could have set the whole island of Oahu ablaze.

A lot of our members think they could have easily come ashore, but I don't know about that. But for a certainty they could have set us afire.

(Author's note: Ken is a onetime president of the Pearl Harbor Survivors Association.)

Prate Stack

◇

Prate Stack was born in North Carolina. However, he was quite young when his family started moving north. He has lived in Fairfield County, Connecticut, for over thirty years and more or less looks at it as his real home.

He was a junior at Yale College in New Haven, Connecticut, when the Japanese bombed Pearl Harbor.

Yes, and life in New Haven in '41 was really great. In one direction we had New York and in the other it was Boston. You could have a tremendous amount of fun on weekends no matter in which direction you chose to go.

All right, Pearl Harbor and the Japanese attack, I just might have been one of the last ones in New Haven to learn that we were at war with Japan. Here's why.

I was a member of the Yale Dramatic Club at the time. We never received as much publicity as the Hasty Pudding Club at Harvard, but we felt our shows were just as good, if not better.

Be that as it may, we were about to go on tour for the first time over the 1941 Christmas holiday. On December 7 we had locked ourselves into one of the Yale halls for a hardworking rehearsal on a show called *Waterbury Tales*. It was a takeoff on Chaucer's *Canterbury Tales*.

That evening, around eight, some guy came running into the hall.

"Jesus Christ," he yelled, "have you heard the news? The goddamn Japs have bombed Pearl Harbor. I don't know where the hell that is, but we're now at war."

Do you know not a one of us could tell him where Pearl Harbor was. Can you believe that? Here's a group of so-called scholars, attending one of the great universities in this country, and none of us knew the location of our country's main naval base in the Pacific. I remember one guy saying the West started in Harrisburg, Pennsylvania. Maybe he was right.

Anyway, I graduated from Yale, went into the Marines, and got shot up pretty bad on Okinawa.

And one more thing. I sure as hell know where Pearl Harbor is now.

1st Lieutenant Steven Saltzman,
91st Coast Artillery

◆

You mentioned the "Old Army." Here's a good case for you. When I was stationed in the U.S., we had an old-timer as first sergeant. Hell, I think he had been in World War I and probably also in the Philippines Insurrection. He had a sign on his desk that read like this:

"Off Limits to Second Lieutenants" and he got away with it. That was the "Old Army."

As for me, I was raised in Wilmington and I graduated from the University of Delaware. While I was a student I enrolled in the ROTC training course and then the advanced military training program. This later got me an extra twenty-one dollars a month. Don't laugh, twenty-one dollars was nothing to sneeze at in the late thirties.

After I graduated, I took a job at an advertising agency. My duties were mainly doing what the other employees didn't want to do. Today they would call me a gofer.

Then in January of '41 I was called into active duty as a lieutenant. I remember walking into that agency with a big smile on my face. I bid them all adieu.

"Good-bye," I said, "I'll see you around." I liked the people, but I hated that crummy job.

Well, they first sent me to Fort Hamilton in Brooklyn. During the train ride we picked up seventy or so other brand-new second lieutenants. They'd come from colleges all over the East. We really had a ball. Rumor had it we'd be joining the 1st U.S. Army Division, but they left Hamilton shortly after we arrived.

At Fort Hamilton I officially became a member of the Coast Artillery Corps, but it seems to me all I did was march troops up and down on the ice. It was colder than a welldigger's ass in Alaska. However, my hour of deliverance was just around the corner.

One morning I was late for work. A bunch of us had been kicking the gong around the night before and I was a bit hungover. I was driving to a meeting when I came to a street pretty well blocked by a moving van. We had been told a new colonel was moving in that morning.

So, what the hell, I figured I'd take a chance. I got around the van by going over the colonel's new lawn.

Oh, hell, by the time I got to the meeting, the new colonel had already put me on report. I guess he was really pissed off. Some of these old-timers could be real chicken shit.

Next came my good fortune. That same morning I received a memo calling for second lieutenants to volunteer for duty in Hawaii. I jumped at the chance.

A few days later I was on my way to Oahu, away from a possible court-martial and those icy Brooklyn streets. I arrived in Hawaii in March of '41.

What a difference! This was the real army. I was a bachelor getting a hundred and seventeen dollars a month and had plenty of free time to spend it.

One of the most pleasant things I was to find out was the way the people who ran the island treated the officers. Remember, this was Hawaii of half a century ago. The line between enlisted men and officers was a lot more stringent than it is now. If you had bars on your shoulders, people like the Castles, Dillinghams, Bishops, and Cooks would open their doors to you, but not to the enlisted men.

All right, let me get this straight. Toward the end of October things started to get more serious. By now I was in the 91st Coast

Artillery at Schofield Barracks. If you have not read James Jones's book *From Here to Eternity*, read it. Because that is quite a realistic picture on what Army life was like on Oahu at the time.

You see, while Jones dwells very much on boxing, and there was a lot of boxing going on at the time, it wasn't just prizefighting. Baseball, football, basketball—there were sports teams for everyone.

Anyway, toward the second week in November, the emphasis was placed more on soldiering. A week or so later we were placed on full alert. We were issued bandoliers filled with cartridges, side arms, rifles, and all that stuff. And our guns were set up in their battle positions all ready for action.

Now, I can't remember just when, but it had to be around the first of December, we were taken off alert. Why, I don't know. I did later hear it was the same all over the island. Naturally, we looked at things in a little different way. You know how it is. You get all geared up for something. Then it's called off. You are bound to think any crisis is over or someone is off his rocker.

Be that as it may. I was going to the University of Hawaii football game against Willamette of Oregon on the sixth of December. I was going with some other officers. I'm sure we would have been partying well into the morning hours, especially since Hawaii won the game. I'm sure I would have ended up sleeping somewhere in Honolulu. This meant I would have been driving back to Schofield just as that first Japanese wave came over.

Remember, they seemed particularly interested in strafing automobiles. I would have been lucky to get back alive.

Anyway, that great pre-war life I had on Oahu was about to change. I ended up spending the night of December 6 at my station.

At this time we were quartered at the very north end of Schofield, near the Kole Kole pass, right next to the mountains. We had these little wooden shacks with screens in our windows. The night of December 6 I more or less spent hanging around the barracks, drank some beer, and went to sleep. To this day I still wonder what kind of a reception we would have given the Japanese the next day if we were still on alert.

The next morning I could hear these airplanes coming from the direction of Kole Kole. Their throttles must have been pulled out because you could hear the planes backfiring. They had to be gliding in.

"The goddamn Navy," I said to myself, "how dare they make so much noise on Sunday morning!"

You see, Sunday morning was somewhat sacred in the pre-war services. You just didn't do things like that.

Then it dawned on me that those airplanes sounded different from anything else I'd ever heard before. I decided to run out to see what was going on. The funny part was I always slept in the nude. There I was, an officer and a gentleman by an act of Congress, standing there looking up at the plane with everything waving in the breeze. Then I looked at the wings of one of the planes. I couldn't believe what I saw.

"Holy shit," I yelled, "those are meatballs!"

I grabbed a beach towel, put it around me, and ran over to Colonel Mitchell's quarters. John Mitchell was our battalion commander. He was a nice old regular army light colonel. He was sound asleep. Might have had a hangover. I burst into his room.

"Colonel, Colonel, wake up. The Japs are attacking us!" He just stared at me with this unbelievable look on his face.

"Blah, blah, blah" is all he could muster. He was so startled he couldn't believe what was going on.

Next, I ran back to my quarters and put on a pair of coveralls but no underwear, my campaign hat but no shoes.

Remember, I was communications officer. What I knew about communications you could put in your ear, but I knew I had to do something. I ran down to the enlisted men's quarters. I had planned on setting up my command post in case of an emergency in an abandoned schoolhouse near Wheeler Field. The walls were about as thick as two sheets of paper.

My crew chief was a soldier named Lowell Klatt, a young fireman from Matawan, New Jersey. Lowell was a great guy, a good soldier, and a firm friend of mine.

Part of my job was to get some ammunition as we'd turned it all in when the alert was recently canceled. We also had to check out the terminal junction boxes for the cable system. I couldn't handle my communications if that was fouled up. All of a sudden this Nakazima showed up. It was flying very low and seemed to be hardly moving.

Somewhere along the line I had grabbed a Springfield rifle. I didn't think the plane was going any more than seventy or eighty miles an hour. I emptied a clip (five rounds) into the plane.

The Nakazima then turned so it would miss this high tension wire. I had quickly put a new clip in the rifle.

Hell, I am an old duck hunter. I had a perfect shot at the pilot. I led the plane for an instant and let him have it. He just slumped over. The plane crashed in back of the schoolhouse. When the attack was over, we went over to see what I had brought down.

It wasn't a very pretty picture. Both the pilot and his machine gunner were dead. The plane had caught fire and the pilot's skin had been burned off his face. I should point out that my wire chief, Lowell Klatt, was also firing, but I do know it was my shot that killed the pilot.

Now, once again, if you have read *From Here to Eternity* or seen the film, you know that Burt Lancaster knocked down a plane with a BAR.

Baloney, there is no way you can hold a BAR in your bare hands like Lancaster did and shoot down anything. You'll burn your hands badly.

However, in the late Gordon Prange's book *At Dawn We Slept*, Prange has both me and Klatt firing BARs when we shot down the plane. Not true. I hit that pilot with a Springfield rifle. I saw him go down.

The next day an officer came over from Army headquarters. He got my crew together.

"All right, men, who shot down the Jap plane?"

A couple of my group spoke up.

"Oh, the lieutenant did. He's a hell of a shot!"

The next thing I knew the colonel had put me up for a DSC. I was amazed. All I did was make a good shot. You don't get the DSC for that. It was later knocked down to a Silver Star. I did accept that and made sure that Klatt got one also.

Well, after the attack there was hell to pay. We were completely caught off our guard. No doubt about that. A while later FDR commissioned a committee to find out why we had been so completely caught with our pants down. It was chaired by a man named Owen Roberts, a justice of the Supreme Court. There was also a retired admiral and our Army general involved, plus a couple of other big shots. They questioned me.

"Lieutenant," they asked, "why do you feel things all seemed to go wrong on December 7?"

"Well," I said, "I feel it was poor leadership." Here's an example. There was a Japanese submarine that used to surface every night to charge its batteries. Hell, they were right offshore. They'd just sit there and thumb their noses at us.

The submarine was just asking for it. We had PBYs flying patrols every night. They could have dropped flares and illuminated the sub in a flash. It would have been duck soup for us.

This was a problem though. Our guns were up on a hill. We'd have to depress the guns below zero if we were going to fire at the sub. The book said this was a no-no. So I went to see the major about it. I told him what I wanted to do. He was flabbergasted.

"Oh, no, Lieutenant, you can't deelevate these guns. Antiaircraft guns are just that, antiaircraft guns."

"Holy Christ," I said, "what the hell difference does it make?"

Oh, he was a major. I was a lowly lieutenant, but I was in trouble. The next morning I dressed up like a toy soldier. I looked just as if I had come out of a bandbox. I marched over to see the chief of Hawaiian artillery. He was a major general. I walked into his office and gave him a snappy salute.

"General," I said, "I'd like to be transferred away from Hawaii."

The general stared at me for a few minutes.

"Why is that, Lieutenant?"

"Because my dog and I are being exposed to unnecessary risks because of the stupidity of your officers."

Then I told him the story. The general chuckled a bit. Then he became real friendly.

"Salty," he said, "you've been on duty all night, right?"

"Yes, sir."

"Well, I've only seen you twice, the other day when I was pinning a Silver Star on you and now. Everyone tells me you're a good man. Go back to your quarters and get a good night's sleep. Let me worry about the regulations."

Anyway, I told the Commission, "If we don't change fast, we just might lose this war."

But, you see, that was the peacetime Army. If the manual said you only fired the guns at aircraft, that's all you did.

I'll tell you one more thing though about the enlisted men who were at Pearl Harbor when the Japanese hit us. My God, they could stretch their dollars! The pay scale was so wretchedly small. Yet they seemed to get by.

I recall one PFC who was a room orderly. He probably could have been promoted, but he didn't want to change jobs. Each payday he'd set up a poker game in one of the rooms with beer and sandwiches. He'd also get a cut of every pot. I later heard he had bought a restaurant in Honolulu out of the money he picked up running those payday games.

Well, I finally left Pearl Harbor and the 91st Coast Artillery. I was transferred to the Army Air Corps where I became a P-38 pilot, but that's another story.

I'll tell you one last thing though. I'll never forget that moment outside of my quarters when I was balls-ass naked. I looked up and saw those Japanese planes coming at me. Talk about a shock! Wow!

The 6th Avenue E

◆

In the fall of 1936 my father drove my brother and me to New York City from Hartford. We were to see the fifth game of the World Series between the New York Yankees and the New York Giants. Dad hated to drive in the city so we parked near the first entrance to the 6th Avenue E and rode that line to Yankee Stadium.

The Yankees were ahead three games to one. The Giants' back was to the wall. Due to a gutsy pitching performance by Hal Schumacher, the Giants won 5-4 in the tenth inning. The Yankees won the Series the next day.

Two years later my dad was reading the Sunday *New York Times*. He turned toward my brother and me.

"Boys, it says here that the 6th Avenue E we rode a couple of years ago has been torn down and sold as scrap iron to Japan. I hope we never get it back in our faces!"

John Gibb had a somewhat similar story to tell about Japan and scrap iron.

In the fall of '41 I was living in Brooklyn, New York, remembered John. As a matter of fact, I was born there in 1922. My parents lived at 2 Montague Terrace, right near the East River. We were on the eighth floor. We could look down on every ship coming into New York City.

The view was tremendous. The Statue of Liberty, the New Jersey shoreline, the bottom of Manhattan, the Brooklyn Bridge, I think we had as good a view as you could get in the five boroughs.

Well, for months I had seen them loading mainly scrap iron into ships flying the Japanese flag. Fifty years is a long strain on a memory, but as I recall, they were doing this right up until the first part of December 1941.

I eventually ended up an ensign in the Navy. I served mainly on a Navy tanker, the U.S.S. *Maumee*. And you can bet that many are the times I have thought of all that scrap iron I'd seen leaving New York Harbor, headed for Japan.

Have a Laugh

◈

In working on my books I have attended dozens of veterans' meetings. I have never met a more sincere and helpful group than the Pearl Harbor Survivors Association. No matter where the meeting, if I was there, I was treated extremely well. They always made me feel welcome.

I'd say the average age of these veterans is between seventy and seventy-one. Their meetings never seem to drag like those of other groups do.

They are always looking for a laugh and most of their humor is aimed at the coming infirmities of age.

Here is a story that one of them told to the meeting at the San Bernardino gathering in California.

"Well," their leader said, "we had a little problem with one of our older members the other day. It was Bill Brown. Bill is eighty-three. He went down to the hospital to make his annual blood deposit. The nurse just shook her head.

" 'I'm sorry, Mr. Brown, I know you have been depositing blood down here for years, but you are now too old to give your blood.'

" 'Oh, my God, nurse, that is awful. Well, I'm here now. Isn't there something I can give?'

"Well, I guess the nurse thought they'd have some fun with old Bill.

" 'Oh, yes,' one of them said, 'take this bottle down to the sperm room. You know what to do. Deposit your sperm in this bottle.'

"So, as the old-timer left, the two nurses were giggling. In fifteen minutes he came back. One of the nurses noticed the empty bottle.

" 'Gee, Mr. Brown, what happened?'

" 'Well, I'll tell you. I pulled it, I rubbed it, and I jerked it.'

"Now there was silence. Then the nurse, trying to control her laughter, spoke.

" 'And?'

" 'I still couldn't get the goddamn top off the bottle!' "

William Anderson, Yeoman Striker,
U.S.S. *Maryland*

◆

I'll tell you something. I was on the U.S.S. *Maryland* on December 7, 1941. I saw what air power could do to battlewagons. That was enough for me. I wanted someplace where I could go and hide. So, I transferred to submarine duty. I could hide there all right, perhaps forever.

But no branch of the Navy played a bigger role in bringing Japan to her knees than the submariners. Our subs sank some 1,113 Japanese merchant ships and 201 naval vessels. How's that for a record!

OK, let's go back to January of '41. I was born in southern California, but as I was starting high school, the family moved to Salina, Oklahoma. As I was over six feet tall and weighed in at a solid 195 pounds, I'm sure that high school coach was glad to see me come to Salina. I sure played a lot of football for him anyway.

So, I graduated in the early summer of '40 and started looking around. But it seems I couldn't find much and I'd usually end up at the local pool hall every afternoon.

What was really depressing though was that there were several guys a year or two older than I who would come down there trying to bum nickels and dimes so that they could shoot a little pool. Hell, just a year or two earlier I'd been playing football with these fellows. Now they were bumming dimes and nickels.

Anyway, I had always been interested in what was going on all over the world. I knew France had fallen and that England was hanging on by her teeth. So, I decided to join the Navy. It just seemed like a pretty good life at the time, plus I was sure we'd be getting into the war raging in Europe before it was over.

All right, if you lived in Salina, you went to Dallas to be sworn into the Navy. I went for the regulars. Someone told me the Reserves were just cannon fodder. I also figured that if we did get into the war, it would be a long one.

So, I was sworn into the Navy and from there we were hustled off to San Diego. Everybody there seemed to be opting for Pearl Harbor, but not me. I'd met this real good-looking young thing, so I put in for yeoman school. A yeoman to me was a guy firing a long bow. I felt it probably meant I'd be a gunner, which was fine with me.

The deal with the girl went fine; they usually did, but the yeoman situation didn't go so well. Hell, all I was was a glorified secretary. I just didn't fit the bill.

Well, I finally was sent out to Pearl aboard an old four-piper. They called it a destroyer-mine sweeper. It was a World War I relic named the U.S.S. *Dorsey*. It surely wasn't as spic and span as the battleships I was to serve on later. If you went down below, you'd see rats as big as tomcats. I had no trouble as long as I stayed above decks, but when I went down to my rack, I could get a little queasy but never really sick. I soon found out I was a pretty good sailor.

When we got to Pearl, I was put on the staff of Admiral Walter Stratton Anderson, a real traveling admiral. He was always moving his flag from one battleship to another.

At first he was on the *West Virginia*. We called it the *Weevie*. Then he moved to the *North Carolina*, which was going back to the States for repairs. We were all in favor of that move because it meant good stateside liberty.

The *North Carolina* was not at Pearl on December 7. I don't know where it was.

We eventually ended up on the *Maryland*, an up-to-date battlewagon. This meant Pearl Harbor and that's where I was when the Japanese hit us.

Liberty at Pearl could be what you made it. I'd frequently rent a bike and cycle all over the island. This was great.

If you got away from Honolulu, the citizens would treat you pretty well. In the city all you stood for was the little money you had in your pocket. Those flesh peddlers on Hotel Street wanted every dime of that.

Speaking of Hotel Street, let me tell you of one of the funniest sights I've ever seen.

Right across from all those countless whorehouses there was a military pro station. It was a good idea to be registered there in case you caught a VD. You could prove you had taken precautions.

OK. The men, and they were from all services, would be given a little tube of this gooey stuff. It was called argyrol.

Across the street from the pro station there was a huge rest room. There were forty urinals on one side of the place and forty urinals on the other side.

You were supposed to take that tube and insert what was in it up your business. You'd put a little bag, like the one you'd get to roll your Bull Durham cigarettes in, over the top of your pecker. You'd drop your pants and your skivvy shorts down to your ankles. Then you would hold your dingus upright for five minutes. This gave that goo a chance to work.

Well, sir, if you walked into that head at 2200 on a Saturday night, you'd see up to eighty men standing over a urinal, shining their moons and patiently waiting for their five minutes to be up. Then they'd haul ass out of that place as fast as they could. Sometimes the whole thing could get ridiculous.

Take the time this young sailor came staggering home to the *Maryland*.

Now, there is nothing that looks any snappier than a clean enlisted man's white Navy uniform. But there is nothing that looks any worse than that same uniform if you've been rolling in the gutter with it.

So, this young sailor, legally he had to be seventeen years of age, but he was probably sixteen, shows up at the gangplank. His uniform is filthy, he has lost his white hat, and he's covered with that cheap purple lipstick the bar girls used to wear.

To top it off he'd been to the pro station and the whole thing was still hanging out with the bag on it.

Fortunately for the kid the OD had a sense of humor. He looked at the youngster.

"Get this clown the hell out of here in a hurry!" he yelled.

And so be it.

Don't let me paint too raunchy a picture though. There were some places where a group of us could go drink. Take the Black Cat, a watering hole over near the YMCA.

Enough about our social life, if you want to call it that. Let's go to the night of December 6. I remember going ashore for a beer and a hamburger. I couldn't afford any more than that at the time.

My battle station was on the bridge with the admiral. Things got so confusing the next day I ended up all over the place.

So, here I am, it was after 0700, the seventh of December. I have grabbed my bucket, filled it with water, unloosened a steam pipe, and let the steam heat work on the water. We didn't have any sinks on the *Maryland*. That was how you'd get the hot water for shaving.

That bucket was really something. Every sailor had his own bucket. You'd put your name on it and by and large nobody would pinch it.

Anyway, I was shaving when the loudspeaker started blaring: "Attention, all hands. General Quarters, General Quarters. This is no shit! The goddamn Nips are here! Once again, this is no shit! Turn to!"

So, I went up on the bridge and there's Admiral Anderson, pacing up and down. He looks like he hadn't been to bed yet. He's got his full dress uniform on. He's pacing back and forth on the bridge with his shoulders hunched forward and his hands behind his back. He is patting them together.

"What to do, what to do, what to do?" he's muttering.

Well, I'm talking to myself in a low voice. "Admiral Anderson, you silly son of a bitch. You're the admiral. If you don't know what to do, how in hell does this Anderson, a yeoman striker, know what to do?"

There was a lieutenant commander by the name of Johnson also there. He seemed to have his wits about him.

"Anderson, go down to the admiral's cabin, get his confidential papers, and bring them up here. And also get his helmet. The admiral has got to have a helmet."

Down I go. Then I got commandeered by another officer.

"Hey, sailor. Take this body down below. The poor guy was killed by that bomb we took. His name was Ensign Crow."

Naturally, I obey the order. The poor guy is bleeding like a stuck pig. Here I am, just nineteen years of age and I'm lugging a corpse down a ladder. And when this corpsman sees me, he's convinced the blood that's all over me is mine.

"All right, sailor, lie down, you're going to be all right. Let me give you a little morphine."

Oh, I had a hell of a time convincing the guy it wasn't my blood.

Anyway, I got Anderson's papers, but I couldn't find his helmet. I picked one up lying on the deck and put it on. Then I ran back up to the admiral.

"Here are your papers, Admiral, as ordered."

Then I got a brainstorm. I'll give my helmet to the admiral. Hell, I might get a Navy Cross. Why not!

So, I said to Mr. Anderson. "Admiral, sir, you don't have a helmet. Here. Take mine."

"Thank you, Anderson, but you don't have one."

"That's all right, sir. I don't matter. You're the admiral. The Navy really needs you!"

"Good thinking, son. You'll hear from me later on."

Believe it or not, I did hear from the admiral about it, but I'll get to that later on.

In the meantime, the first wave is past and the second wave of planes has started. As it turned out, we had taken a bomb right through the enlisted men's head. I've got to take a crap so badly I was bouncing from one leg to another.

Incidentally, you never hear about things like this, but if you're ever constipated, go find an air raid. I found out later on everyone literally had the crap scared out of them.

So, I was right near a head in officers' country. The hell with it, I wasn't going to let go in my pants. I opened the hatch and went into forbidden country.

I locked the door and settled down. Then came a knocking on the hatch.

"Hey, hurry up!" the guy yelled.

"Just a minute."

"God damn it, hurry up!"

So, I quickly finished, pulled up my pants, and opened the door.

Holy Christ, there is a four-striper standing there!

"Outta my way!" he yelled. He pushes me aside. He had his trousers unbuckled before he sat down.

The next thing I heard was a groan.

"Just made that one," he sighed.

I got my ass outta there as quickly as I could. I never heard a word about it.

The four-striper was named Nick Carter. He was a colorful character. He was born at sea. His dad was a merchant captain. They could take their wives aboard with them. Nick had been born on one of his dad's cruises.

Nick was bald as a cucumber and his face was really weather-beaten. It looked as if he was always looking into a nor'easter.

The admiral was cut from the same cloth, but he didn't appear to be as savvy as Carter.

I can remember the two of them standing on the bridge one time. The admiral turned to Carter.

"Nick, what do you make the wind velocity to be?"

Nick sniffed the air.

"About eight knots, Admiral," he replied.

"You're crazy; it's only about six. Quartermaster, give us the wind velocity."

A little later the quartermaster came back.

"About eight knots, Admiral."

Carter just laughed and rubbed a finger on his nose.

OK. Back to Carter, rushing into the head. If you ever wanted to realize what the saying "Rank has its privileges" means, just look at the enlisted men's head and the officers'. We had a trough with running water. The officers had a sit-down toilet that flushed. They had sinks; we had our buckets. All in all they were as different as night and day.

Well, we didn't fare so badly, due to the *Oklahoma* being outboard to us. I don't know how many torpedoes the *Okie* took, but she was on her side and there was no way any torpedoes were going to get through her and hit us. All in all, I guess you can say we didn't get hit too hard, especially in regard to the *Arizona* and the *Oklahoma*, but, of course, it was hard enough for Ensign Crow and his family.

So, not long after the attack, I was called into the admiral's stateroom. I spruced myself up as pretty as possible, walked into his quarters, and saluted.

"Yeoman Striker Anderson reporting as ordered, sir."

"Anderson, sit down. Tell me where does your branch of the Anderson clan hail from?"

I told him. It was doubtful that we were related. Then he thanked me, giving me the helmet. Oh, boy, here comes the medal, I thought.

"Tell me, young man, did you graduate from high school?"

"Yes, sir, just a year ago last summer."

"Then how would you like to go to the Naval Academy?"

"Very much so, sir."

"All right, we're heading back to the States for repairs soon. We'll have you bone up on math and sciences. Then we'll get you a test. You do well and you'll get in the Academy. They always take some men from the fleet each year."

Well, I was feeling pretty good, but my number one weakness was going to haunt me again. As for getting back to the States, that sounded great. The harbor was beginning to stink of oil and other things. So, we took off for Seattle, Washington.

When we arrived, the powers that be had arranged for me to have liberty every night so I could go to night school.

Then came the problem. I met this beautiful young woman. Every night I'd sign in at the school, but I didn't go. The arms of this young lady were a hell of a lot more appealing than geometry. When it came time to take the test, I owned up to what had been going on.

Oh, boy, was Admiral Anderson ever hot under the collar! He called me every name in the book, but what the hell, I was always a sucker for a cute young thing.

Shortly afterward, I transferred to the submarines. I go to as many of the underwater reunions as I can. Those are real barn burners!

The Torpedoes

Historians have no definite idea how long Yamamoto nurtured the idea of an attack on Pearl Harbor. We do know that one problem he had was the depth of the water at Pearl. The harbor was too shallow for successful torpedo runs.

So, in November of 1940 the British Navy played a part in Yamamoto's decision. The British sent twenty-one carrier-based planes into Taranto harbor in Italy. They torpedoed and sank three Italian battleships while losing just three planes.

Yamamoto immediately called for all the details of the daring British raid. For openers, the Japanese admiral wanted to know how deep the water was in Taranto harbor. The answer was forty-two feet. As Pearl Harbor's depth was forty-five feet, the good admiral was very interested. How was it done?

The British had used special torpedoes because conventional torpedoes were useless in such shallow water.

How did you get such torpedoes?

It was all in the fins. One rigged the fins so they would run straight and not "porpoise" in shallow water. It was as simple as that. From then on Yamamoto was dead set on a Pearl Harbor attack.

The news on the British attack also amazed Washington, D.C. A man who I believe was greatly underrated, Frank Knox, also called for a complete report on the Taranto affair. When he found out the water depth in Italy, he sent the following memo to the Army Secretary, Henry Stimson.

"The success of the British aerial torpedo attack against ships at anchor suggests that precautionary measures be taken immediately to protect Pearl Harbor against such a surprise attack in the event of war between the United States and Japan."

Apparently nothing came of it, but once again, bully for the old Rough Rider.

Robert Van Sant

◆

Bob Van Sant was raised in Baltimore, Maryland. During World War II he saw considerable rough service as a tanker in Burma. He remembers Pearl Harbor vividly.

I was with a close friend of mind named Frank Getz and several others. Frank is now a retired Air Force colonel. We'd had a great time watching Slinging Sammy Baugh lead the Redskins to a 20-14 victory over the Philadelphia Eagles. Baltimore wasn't in the NFL then and the Washington-Philadelphia rivalry was a big thing.

After the game we went over to Washington Boulevard and headed for Rely, Maryland, where we lived. As we got close to home I noticed that I was low on gas. I pulled into Al's Esso station. We all used to get a big kick out of Al.

Normally he would ask us what we wanted but not this time. He came over to us with an amazed look on his face.

"Holy shit, Mr. Van Sant, those bastard Japs have bombed Vanilla."

"No, Al, you must mean Manila."

"Manila, Vanilla, who cares? They bombed it. We're at war."

Just then, someone from another car yelled over.

"Al means Pearl Harbor in Hawaii. It's true. The Japs did a job on Pearl this morning."

My first reaction was shock. And I haven't liked the bloody Japanese since.

Then I thought some more. I had just been summarily kicked out of Washington and Lee University. I had been wondering what I would do. Now I knew. I was going to enlist in the Army Air Corps. I tried the next day, but it was no soap. My eyes weren't good enough.

Well, there had been Van Sants in every war this country had been in, going back to the American Revolution. My family had been on both sides in the American Civil War.

Anyway, I ended up in the China-Burma-India Theater, fought the good war, came home, married, went into the paper business, and raised a family. But I will never forget Al saying that the "Japs had bombed Vanilla."

John McCaran, U.S.S. *Arizona*

You know, it was many years after the *Arizona* went down before I could talk about the Pearl Harbor attack. I would completely lose control if I tried. After all, we lost some eleven hundred men out of fifteen hundred there. I probably could remember hundreds of them if I could see their faces, but I am afraid that matching the face with a name is gone forever.

Others, who were good friends of mine, will stay with me till I chuck it in. Take Worth Lightfoot. He was not only in the 6th Division with me but he was also on my gun mount. As Kipling put it in one of his poems: "Many a pint we shared."

Lightfoot ended up in the same base hospital as I did after December 7. I got a chance to see him, but I could quickly tell he wasn't going to make it. It seems that when the big explosion occurred, fire had actually gotten into his lungs. They were burned beyond help.

But Lightfoot is only one memory. I can't tell you how many times over the last fifty years I have asked myself the same question: "Why were all those shipmates of mine killed and not me?" Who the hell knows?

There is one thing that happened in 1963 that helped to shake me out of my doldrums. One of our ship's bells had ended up somewhere back in the States. They decided it belonged at Pearl with the *Arizona* memorial.

So, they set up a ceremony, honoring the return of the bell to its ship. I was stationed at Pearl so they asked me to unveil the bell at the proper time. The main speaker was a Marine general named Krulak. He is one hell of a guy!

Everything went like clockwork as we placed the bell back where it belonged. We have quite a memorial there on the top of my old ship. There are some eight hundred of my shipmates entombed there with another three hundred or so at the Punch Bowl Cemetery.

Well, shortly after the *Arizona* went down, they decided they'd have divers go down and start bringing the bodies up. But, hell, it was awful down there.

I knew one of the divers. His name was Daniel. He had been a member of the *Arizona*'s crew a short time before the attack. He told me that he had found a dead friend of his down there. The body was so bloated he had to cut the corpse open to get it up. I don't know if he went down again after that, but I know he was all shaken up about it.

So, they kept going down but finally decided they'd leave the rest of the bodies down there with their beloved *Arizona* forever. They belonged there.

One more thing. They say Pearl Harbor meant the end of the battleship era. They are right. But it was also the end of the old Navy. When I was sent on active duty in '37, there were only about seventy thousand men in the Navy. We were going to need one hell of a lot more than that if we were going to defeat the Japanese.

OK, let's go back to the beginning. I was a poor Irish kid from Saugus, Massachusetts. My father died when I was three. Mother eventually remarried, but there was never enough money around. My mother was a saint.

Well, I joined a U.S. Naval Reserve unit at Lynn. I received a small amount of money for each meeting. The next year I was eighteen years old so I figured I'd go into the regulars, but it wasn't as easy as I thought it would be. You had to be physically perfect. I mean, number one. It wasn't until 1940 that the Navy started to expand. When the war did start, we had a smaller navy than the Japanese.

In the fall of '37 they sent me to boot camp in Newport, Rhode Island. My company commander was an old salt named Charlie Cruise. He was all Navy and a yard wide. They don't make 'em like Charlie anymore.

Listen to this. We were at parade one day and someone really goofed off. Wow, was Cruise pissed off! He used to walk with a saber. He threw that sword down on the parade ground. It bounced back up and cut his lip.

Wow, now all hell broke out. He marched us back to our quarters and we had to turn out with our sea bags and hammocks. In those days you slept on hammocks. We had to duck waddle all over the parade grounds for an hour. Some of the guys were actually passing out.

Boot camp was all over the first of December. I received a ten-day furlough. After that things moved fast. I put in for the U.S.S. *Vincennes*, a brand-new cruiser, but I didn't get it. The *Vincennes* went down off Guadalcanal in August of 1942. Those Japanese sailors were tough cookies.

Shortly afterward I was assigned to the U.S.S. *Arizona* at Long Beach, California. I can tell you that exact date when I went aboard her. It was March 3, 1938.

So, this was to be my home for the next three years and eight months. And if you were in the battleship Navy in those days, you loved your ship, or at least I did.

Anyway, you know what they say, that first real girlfriend is always something special. It's the same with a sailor's first ship. Part of me will always be with those guys entombed with their ship in Pearl Harbor.

Well, sometime in 1940 we got the word that either President Roosevelt or the secretary of the Navy, Franklin Knox, wanted the Pacific Fleet to move from California to Pearl Harbor. From then on we were in and out of Honolulu constantly, usually for about thirty days.

But when we'd get back to Pearl, most of my shipmates were raring to go. I can remember one time when we were at a bar called the Black Cat. Some of our boys were definitely three sheets to the wind. One of these guys spoke up.

"Listen, you're not a real sailor until you get a tattoo."

That turned the conversation around to the various types of tattoos. We all said it would be great to have U.S.S. *Arizona* on our arms. Someone also mentioned "Death Before Dishonor, Mother, Barbara" (his girlfriend), things like that.

"OK," that guy said, "let's go over to that Chinaman's place and find out how much a tattoo would cost. His joint is over near Hotel Street. We can at least look into it." So, off we went.

It was a Saturday night and the tattoo parlor was busy as hell. We had to stand in line. You know how much patience you have when you're half in the bag. Most of us really didn't want to do it anyway. Finally we said the hell with it. But you can rest assured we needled that guy who really wanted the tattoo for weeks. I'm pretty sure he was killed on December 7.

You know, it is hard to explain the camaraderie that existed among the crew of a ship like the *Arizona*.

For instance, there were four of us that used to share a locker at the Uptown Locker Club. We could keep our civilian clothes there when we went ashore. Let's see. There was Pearson, I know he was later killed, Hilton, and another sailor named Bud Weiss.

So, one day we had all gone to a bar called Schuyler's. This was the favorite watering hole for the men on the *Arizona* and the *Saratoga*. Most of the ships had their favorite bars like that.

Hell, we were sitting there having a drink when I saw a sailor giving this girl a real hard time. All of a sudden he hauled off and really smacked the girl, knocking her over.

Well, she was a particularly good friend of mine. I decided to be a hero. Haw! Haw! I jumped over to their table, pulled the guy out of his chair, and gave him my best shot.

Oh, boy! This guy went ass over teakettle on his backside. I really cold cocked him. See this scar on my knuckle. I got that on that night.

Then my buddies turned to. They got me out of that bar hell bent for election. We moved on to another spot.

Christ, the next day it was all over the ship about one of our guys flattening a sailor from the *Saratoga* over at Schuyler's.

And that wasn't all. It seems the guy I had hit turned out to be a onetime welterweight champion of the fleet.

This was a shock. I was no boxer. In a stand-up battle this guy would have killed me. From then on I stayed out of Schuyler's when the *Saratoga* was in port. I never ran into this guy again. But I certainly continued to go ashore with my pals.

Whatever, I certainly liked girls but not the pros on Hotel Street or those tough amateurs who waited for the fleet to come in.

During peacetime you could bring guests aboard on Sundays. That's when we'd see the officers and their young ladies, who looked as if they had just gotten out of finishing school, touring the ship. And then we had the old salts bringing their Battleship Bettys aboard.

We had a boatswain named Susco. He was a real tough guy and a hell of a ladies' man. He thought so anyway. He had invited these two Amazons to come aboard one Sunday. He knew I had a special girl back in Saugus and that I was planning to get married. So, he detailed me to show them around the ship. What a pain in the backside, but Susco thought it was funny.

I ran into the chief again at the end of the war. The Navy had him at the Chelsea Naval Hospital outside of Boston, drying out. I guess he'd turned into an alcoholic. He was tough all right, but he was one hell of a sailor. I hope he snapped out of it.

But when it's all said and done, the things I remember most about those peacetime Navy days were those bull sessions we'd have, especially on Wednesday afternoons and Sundays. A group of us gun strikers would meet on the boat deck with a few quarts of ice cream. I think we paid thirty cents a quart for it at the Gee Dunk shop. We would sit there and rap. We'd talk mainly about girls, sports, hometowns, anything you could think of. You could get as close as brothers during these sessions. Maybe that's why I took December 7 so badly and clammed up for so long.

But when I did start talking about it, for some reason it made things a lot easier. Oh, I still remember those men who were lost, I always will, but it's not as devastating as it used to be.

OK. Now for December 7. When the cry "General Quarters, this is no drill!" sounded, everyone turned to. We just did what we were trained to do. We acted by rote. A thousand men acted at once. I'm sure none of them had the slightest idea they only had a few minutes of life left.

At the time I was standing muster, getting ready to go ashore for Shore Police duty. I immediately ran up the ladder to my five-incher at gun mount seven. Lightfoot was already there and had removed the safety latch.

Now, here's one for you. I went over to the ammunition place and removed my neckerchief. Then I calmly folded it just as if I had come off liberty and was going to put it back in my locker. Then I put it on the ammunition ready box.

There were four of us on mount seven. But to this day I can't remember who the pointer and trainer were, but they were there also. I opened up the ammunition, loaded three rounds into the fuse box, and cranked them in.

From here on it gets rather foggy. I could see the explosion happening, but, as I remember, couldn't hear it. Then I saw a blinding flash. It was gigantic. The next thing I knew I was in the water. When in the hospital, I asked around to find out what had happened (of course, I knew my ship had been sunk but that was all), here is what I found out.

It seems that at least one bomb had landed alongside of number two turret. Apparently it penetrated the fuel storage. A ton of highly inflammable explosives was also hit. The power ignited, blasting throughout the ship, culminating with the loudest bang known to man. As I have said, I don't even remember hearing it.

When they told me I had been picked up by a motor launch,

some of my memory came back. I could remember the wounded and the blood that was all over the boat. The bay was quickly filling up with oil.

And the dead. They were everywhere. Sometimes I'd see a face that I recognized. Mercifully, I passed out again and didn't awaken till I was in the hospital.

Another thing I was told was that Admiral Kidd (he had moved his flag to the *Arizona*) was killed by the blast as was Franklin Van Valkenburg, our skipper at the time. Kidd was the first American admiral to be killed in action, even though one was also killed at Savo Bay a year or so later.

Well, sometime after Christmas I felt well enough to go back to sea. I figured they'd put me in the ship's sick bay for a while, but it wasn't to be. I ended up on a destroyer. It was a lot different from the *Arizona*. I spent the rest of the war there.

I did get back to battleship duty during the Korean War, serving on the mighty *Missouri*.

Between Regular and Reserve service I spent a total of thirty-three years in the naval service. Twenty of these years were on sea duty.

OK. Our two-hour chat has revolved around Pearl Harbor. Let me leave you with a light touch. There was a joke floating around Oahu after the attack. It seems that a badly wounded seventeen-year-old Marine PFC was lying in bed at the hospital at Aiea.

The doctor came over to his bedside.

"How're you doing, son?" he said.

"Oh, I'm going to be all right, sir. But yuh know, ah didn't even know them Japs was mad at us."

And those are my feelings exactly.

Praise the Lord and Pass the Ammunition

◆

Andy Gura was another young lad who joined the U.S. Naval Reserve in 1940 with communications as his specialty.

After a year of schooling in communications, he was sent to Pearl Harbor where he went aboard the U.S.S. *New Orleans*, a light cruiser, and there he stayed until the end of the coming war.

He had originally volunteered for a year of active duty but when his tour of duty was up in November of 1941, they were not discharging Reservists. He remembers December 7 of '41 as if it were yesterday.

Well, on the morning of the attack we were at Pearl Harbor for repairs. Our main engine was all apart so we couldn't get under way. When we spotted those meatballs the thing for us to do was go to our battle stations. We got our five-inchers and our machine guns going in a big hurry. I really don't know for sure if we hit anything or not. I do remember watching some Japanese planes going down that we had been firing at.

Our ship's chaplain was an officer named Howell M. Forgy. When he heard General Quarters, he ran over to our five-inchers. The men had set up a chain gang passing up the ammunition. The chaplain saw this and he shouted, "Praise the Lord and pass the ammunition." And whenever they'd slack off, he'd yell again, "Praise the Lord and pass the ammunition." This went on until the second wave of Japanese planes had passed.

Well, you can bet it spread throughout the fleet how a sky pilot had been the cheerleader for the gunners on the *New Orleans*. The next thing we knew some news reporters had sent the story back to the States.

A song composer named Frank Loesser heard the tale. He put together a song about it.

Of course, Forgy didn't do any gunning. Chaplains don't do that.

But I really can't remember many outstanding songs that came out of World War II. I guess "Praise the Lord and Pass the Ammunition" is as good as any. And it all came from the good old *New Orleans*.

Or So They Say

History is full of statements that live long after they are made. Some are not even made, but they still live. Whatever, many of them are colorful as can be. And some of them are attributed to more than one person. Here are five of my favorites connected with the events leading up to and including the Pearl Harbor attack.

One remark was apparently made by at least two people. On the night of December 6, 1941, Commander Roscoe F. Good, USN, looked out over a brilliantly lit up Pearl Harbor.

"What a beautiful target that would make!" he said.

A few hours later Lt. General Walter C. Short, U.S. Army, was driving home with his wife. They had been to a party at the Schofield Officers' Club. As they drove by the harbor, Short was also impressed by the brilliant sight of the giant warships.

"What a target that would make!" he said.

It can be assumed that at 7:55 the next morning Commander Mitsuo Fuchida looked down on the blue-watered harbor and said the same thing.

At 8:15 A.M. Admiral Husband Kimmel was also looking out at the harbor. The *Oklahoma* had just rolled over. At that moment a spent bullet came through the window and struck Kimmel's blouse. He picked up the slug and studied it.

"It would have been more merciful if it had killed me!" lamented the good admiral. He knew that right or wrong, he would get the majority of the blame for the surprise attack.

A third statement that will live in history was made by Yamamoto himself, the reluctant architect of the Japanese attack. When his young officers cheered him, he pointed out the emptiness of the victory without the sinking of any carriers.

"Gentlemen, I'm afraid all we have done is awaken a sleeping giant and filled him with a terrible resolve."

Bill Halsey was another media man's delight. Very quotable. After being ordered to deliver eight planes to Wake Island, he questioned Admiral Kimmel.

"What should I do if I run into any Japs?"

Kimmel mused for a few seconds. "Bill, use your own common sense."

Halsey chuckled. "That's the best damn order I ever received."

On his way back delivering those planes Halsey surveyed the devastated Pearl Harbor. Then he roared.

"When we're through with those bastards, the only place the Japanese language will be spoken will be in hell!"

Vincent Vlack

Vince Vlack spent over four years aboard the U.S.S. *Arizona*. By pure chance he was not aboard her on December 7, 1941. His bride had recently come to Pearl Harbor. Vin was spending a weekend ashore.

As a matter of fact, Yeoman 1st Class Vlack has to be one of the luckiest sailors in the history of the United States Navy.

When he reenlisted in the Navy in 1941, he was almost sent to Admiral Hart's Asiatic fleet. This was a small body of ships thousands of miles away from any other Americans. Almost all hands were either killed or captured.

However, instead of going to Admiral Hart's command he returned for a second tour of duty on the *Arizona*.

And finally in 1943 he went aboard the U.S.S. *Gambier Bay*. She went down off the Philippines. Once again he was not aboard.

So, Mr. Vlack, I advise you not to play the state lottery. You have run out of luck.

Today Vince lives in Anaheim with his wife of some fifty years. He is more or less the historian of the *Arizona*.

"I used to dread going back to Pearl," he said to me. "All those shipmates sleeping underneath that memorial and I wasn't even aboard when she went down. After fifty years it is nowhere as bad, but I still get a lump in my throat when I salute the monument."

I am sure that they didn't know it at the time, but the Marines on Wake Island avenged the dead of the *Arizona*. The pilot who was credited with dropping the bomb that caused the monstrous explosion on the Arizona was Petty Officer Noboru Kanai. Kanai in turn was shot down at Wake Island.

As it was, almost all the Japanese pilots who bombed Pearl were eventually killed in World War II.

Even Admiral Isoroku Yamamoto was killed by American planes off Bougainville in 1943. Although he was not at Pearl Harbor during the attack, he was in overall command.

The man who was the field commander of the task force that went to Pearl was Vice-Admiral Chuichi Nagumo. His photograph stares out at me from World War II books as if he were a pugnacious bulldog.

Whatever, he either died by his own hands or in a banzai charge on the island of Saipan.

It was also the American victory at Saipan that caused the downfall of General Hideki Tojo, premier of Japan. He was later hanged as a war criminal. Tojo had to sanction the attack on Pearl Harbor.

As a matter of fact, one of the few Japanese involved in the Pearl Harbor attack to survive the war was Commander Mitsuo Fuchida, leader of the air attack itself. After many close calls with death, he converted to Christianity and died in bed at age seventy-three.

And let's not forget Midway. The four carriers sunk at Midway in early June were all involved in the Pearl Harbor attack.

We may have shot down just twenty-nine pilots at Pearl, but the Pearl Harbor pilots were the best they had. In addition, they lost several more good pilots at Wake.

Then came the Coral Seas and Midway. It was indeed a rare Japanese who took part in the Pearl Harbor attack who was still alive in August of '45.

All right, in 1937 I was living in Ravenna, Nebraska, when I decided to go into the Navy. A boyhood chum of mine, Elmer Pershing Schlund, was a machinist's mate 1st class in A Division on the *Arizona*. I thought it would be great to have Elmer as a shipmate. Some three hundred or so sailors from the *Arizona* survived the Japanese attack. My friend Elmer was not one of them.

All right, I went aboard the *Arizona* in August of '37. It was on the West Coast then.

Well, in March of '40 I married a hometown girl named Jeanne. We're still married, which is a little unusual these days.

At this time the Japanese were becoming a problem. Washington figured they'd move most of our battleships to Pearl Harbor. They told us it would be for a six-week cruise. Then it was extended to six months.

They kept adding six months each time. It became apparent that Pearl was going to be our home port, at least as long as we could not come to some type of understanding with the Japanese.

So, in August of '40 my wife borrowed some money from her uncle, got a ticket on a steamer named the *Matsonia*, and came to Honolulu.

Now, not too many enlisted men were married at this time, not at Pearl anyway. I had made yeoman 1st class by then. I also had a ship service job so I made a little bit more than my regular pay grade, but it was still tough to get along. My wife was going to get a job the first of the year, which would sure help.

All right, I had gone ashore on the night of December 6. My wife was living then in an apartment on Waikiki Beach. Our closest neighbor was a chief petty officer on the U.S.S. *Curtis*. Around eight o'clock in the morning of the seventh his wife banged on our door and yelled: "I just heard on the radio that the Japs were bombing Pearl. You'd better get up!"

We got up in a flash and turned our radio on. The program was all about the attack.

"This attack is the real McCoy. All servicemen return to your stations at once," blared from the radio.

I put my uniform on as quickly as I could. There were five others in that same complex that were from the *Arizona*. All six of us took off for Pearl as quickly as we could. We headed for the trolley that took us to the YMCA, right across from the Black Cat. There we flagged down a cab. When that driver heard we were from the *Arizona*, he started really moving. When we got out of the center of town, he put that pedal on the floor. It seemed funny as hell driving that fast, but there was practically no traffic.

When we arrived at the main gate, the Marine sentry told us to go to the receiving station. We did, but there was nobody there.

So, we went to Merry's Point Landing. Here we had a good look at the destruction even though there was so much black smoke that visibility was quite limited. I did have a good view of the capsized *Oklahoma*, which saddened me greatly.

At this point a Japanese plane came in very low. We could see this grinning pilot as plain as day. It was a bomber and his machine gunner was having trouble adjusting his gun so he could blast whoever was standing around. There must have been a hundred and fifty or so of us.

And do you know that grinning pilot made a complete turn around and came back!

Well, maybe that machine gunner's weapon was jammed. He sure as hell seemed to be working on his gun ferociously, but he never fired a shot.

However, there was a big pile of rocks where we were. As the pilot came back, and remember he was flying real low, everyone started to throw rocks at the plane. It was futile, of course.

But perhaps that pilot gave a second thought to men who would try to fight airplanes with rocks. Such people, particularly as they represented the mightiest industrial power in the world, were going to be pretty hard to beat.

Anyway, it seems to me that the plane with the grinning pilot crashed over near the hospital area. Maybe one of those rocks hit him in the head, but I doubt it.

Pretty soon a motor launch pulled into Merry's Point Landing.

It was loaded with wounded sailors. I recognized one of them. He seemed to know me. He kinda grinned and said, "*Arizona*" as he offered me his arm in a gesture to help him ashore.

Of course I did. I didn't realize he was bleeding as much as he was, but the horrifying thing was part of his burnt skin came off in my hand. I hope he made it, but I wouldn't bet on it.

Now for the clincher. After a while we thought we'd get some breakfast in the galley. The master-at-arms at the receiving station took one look at the blood on my uniform.

"As you were, sailor," he yelled. "You can't come in here like that. Get ahold of a clean uniform and come back. You look like a bum not a sailor."

Oh, I got a pair of dungarees that were four sizes too big for me and I hunted up a T-shirt somewhere. I couldn't find a belt so I had to tie my pants up with a line that was hanging around somewhere. I surely didn't look like a parade-ground sailor, but I did get fed.

Well, I never did get aboard my battleship again. However, I was a long way from through with the *Arizona*. One glance at my ship was enough to tell me the *Arizona* must have suffered hundreds of casualties.

As a matter of fact, we had over eleven hundred dead, which comes out to roughly seventy-eight percent of the crew. Our defense never really got going.

Oh, I don't think it would have made any difference. The Japanese surprise was complete, but I don't think the directors on our antiaircraft guns were up to the Japanese speed. A good deal of our equipment was old.

Remember, the American economy was just beginning to come out of a deep depression. Naval budgets were tight. It was just a year or so before December 7 that we didn't have enough sailors to man all our guns in a General Quarters drill. Men would shift around from battle station to battle station.

Whatever, you can take anyone from the *Arizona* who was not on board that Sunday (and most of the men were on board) and ask him if he lost any pals and he'll have to answer, "Yes." Along with my boyhood friend, Elmer, I lost plenty of other friends.

One of them was named Lon Storm. He was also married. Lon Storm's enlistment was going to be up in January. His wife was pregnant so he was not going to reenlist. As he was a yeoman 1st class, I knew I was going to miss him greatly. They had even closed their apartment in Oahu. I can't remember why he wasn't ashore that Sunday, but unfortunately he stayed on the *Arizona*. Before things got so touchy with the Japanese, all the battleships had a football team. Lon Storm was our fullback and I think he was the best runner in that battleship league we had. I don't know if he's entombed in the ship or if his body was brought up.

You see, many people think that all 1,177 men killed are still on the *Arizona*. This is not true. Right up to August of '43 they were pumping out compartments and bringing up remains. It was really tough, particularly with all that oil still down there.

One of the divers was a warrant officer who had been on the *Arizona*. This is what he told me.

"Gee, Vin, you couldn't see well at all with all that oil. I'd just stand still and eventually a skeleton would float by and tap me on the shoulder. Of course, I couldn't tell who he was, but he was probably someone I had known. Hell, we could have drunk beer together at the Black Cat or somewhere. It was horrible."

In the long run it was too much for the warrant officer. He became a falling-down drunk. He did join AA, however.

So, they figure at the latest count there are some 945 sailors whose whereabouts are unknown. But there are another sixty unknown bodies at the Punch Bowl Cemetery. At least half of those are probably *Arizona* men. What that means is that there are still 915 sailors aboard that sunken ship. May they rest in peace.

Now for a bad omen. Five weeks before the attack when we were out to sea, another battleship was coming in at us on the port side. Both ships didn't seem to realize what was happening until the last minute. The other ship had reciprocating engines, very powerful. It had been headed right toward our wardroom.

Anyway, there was no collision. My God, what a mess that would have been! The other ship was the U.S.S. *Oklahoma*. If there had been a crash, both ships would have been damaged so badly they would have been taken back to the West Coast for repairs.

Anyway, as I am sure you know, the *Arizona* and the *Oklahoma* were the only two battleships that were knocked out of World War II completely.

Now, let me ask you a question. You have talked to scores of men who were at Pearl during the attack. Has anyone else mentioned the battle of the bands on December 6?

"Yes, several sailors."

Who the hell won it?

"No one seems to know."

Well, I am not even sure the *Arizona* was in the finals, but I'd surely like to know who won.

"I'll tell you if I find out."

Well, on the sixth of December my wife and I were with Lee Crothers, a buddy of mine. His wife Edith had arrived in Pearl on the fifth. She had come to Honolulu on the U.S.S. *Henderson*, a well-known American transport. As I recall, we had a welcoming party for Edith at the Royal Hawaiian.

A man named Everett Reed, who lived in the same apartment complex as we did, was also at the Hawaiian. It was his birthday and we all went over to his table to give him our best wishes.

I tell you this because both Crothers and Reed also served on the *Arizona*. Poor Crothers, he served throughout the war and just before it ended he was doing Shore Police duty in Manila. He was killed in an accident during the V-J celebration.

All right, here is a picture I took of my wife, an *Arizona* sailor named Howard Watson, and his wife, Rose. Howard was yet another man not aboard our ship when the attack came. I think there were about forty of us who can thank God we were ashore that night.

This picture was taken at the docks in November of '41. That ship in the background was the *Tio Maru*. Not a bad picture if I do say so myself. It was taken by a ten-dollar Brownie.

In checking the records after the war I found out that the *Tio Maru* was a Japanese spy ship. When I took that picture, the *Tio Maru* had just finished a trip over the exact same route Nagumo's task force was to take in December. The spy ship had not been detected and neither was Nagumo.

Oh, here's an interesting policy. Any of us who were serving aboard the *Arizona* on December 7 but were not actually aboard can have our ashes scattered about the fallen ship when we die. But any survivor who was aboard ship when the Japanese attacked can have his ashes actually buried in the ship with his dead shipmates.

Have no doubts about it, the crew of the *Arizona* was in many ways like a huge family. I attended the ceremony when the remains of Bosun 2nd Class Ramon John Teal were laid to rest with his shipmates.

Of course, there were also some real family aboard, thirty-four sets of brothers to be exact. Of the brothers there were three sets of three brothers and in each case two of the three were KIA. We also had a father and son aboard. Their name was Frees. Both were lost. And among the brothers we had one set of twins. Their name was Anderson. One of them was lost. Actually, I am quite sure that of the thirty-four brothers, at least one was lost in each case.

Well, there is one ugly rumor that has been floating around for years that I'd like to kill right now. What I am talking about is the allegation that many of our crew were either drunk or ashore on Sunday morning, December 7. That is such a viciously untrue statement that I wouldn't even mention it if I hadn't heard it so many times.

Well, of the entire crew of the *Arizona*, just about one hundred percent of the men were aboard and had been there since 2200 hours of the previous night. The only exception I know of were the forty married men who were on a legitimate weekend pass.

The official report also states that thirty-seven of our officers were also aboard on the night of December 6 and were on call when General Quarters was sounded.

What happened is the Japanese attack was totally unexpected and deadly.

Oh, they paid for it all right, but that couldn't help our honored dead.

The Battlewagons

◆

With no carriers at Pearl Harbor the Japanese soon centered in on the eight battleships docked at Pearl. Actually, nine, if you count the *Utah*. This old warrior had been reduced to the role of a training ship and was hardly a first-class combat vessel. However, it was treated like a battlewagon of the line by the Japanese. They sent it to the bottom along with sixty-four sailors of its crew.

The story of the eight remaining is really a testimony to what the U.S. Navy can do with its back against the wall.

First the *Arizona*. It was decided that she was too far gone to be refloated. What is left of this gallant old sea dog is still at Pearl. It serves as a memorial to the memory of not only her crew but to all hands of all services who died on that beautiful December morning half a century ago.

Next the *Oklahoma*. On inspection after the attack it first seemed beyond repair. It did have to be moved to clear her berth at Pearl. Eventually she was removed and refloated.

In December of 1956 the job of hauling the *Oklahoma* back to the States began. There she was to be sold for scrap iron. Halfway between Pearl and California they ran into a storm. The towline broke and the *Oklahoma* went to the bottom of the Pacific.

When this news was flashed back to Pearl Harbor, it was greeted with great rejoicing. None of the Pearl Harbor veterans wanted to see their old ship sold for junk. Better to see their "*Okie*" go to Davey Jones's locker than to be turned into scrap iron.

Now for the other ships. The *Pennsylvania, Maryland*, and *Tennessee* were all on their way to the States before Christmas of '41. All three featured prominently in the remaining naval actions throughout the war.

The *Nevada, California*, and *West Virginia* needed a good deal of work. While they all had been reported sunk by the Japanese, this simply was not true. It did take a minor miracle to get them back to sea, but it did happen.

As for the *Nevada*, Admiral Nimitz took a look at her and shook his head.

"That ship will never sail again," he said.

But he didn't reckon with the expertise of the Pearl Harbor Repair and Salvage Unit. They had the *Nevada* under her own steam by the end of April. The *Nevada* helped silence Nazi guns at Normandy and was at anchor in Tokyo harbor in September of '45.

The *California* needed major repairs. She left Pearl Harbor in the fall of '42 and headed for Puget Sound in the state of Washington. Completely overhauled, she returned to the Pacific and had won seven battle stars by the end of the war.

Last we have the *West Virginia*, or as she was called, the *Weevie*. Only the *Arizona* and the *Oklahoma* had taken a worse pounding. But once again it was the Pearl Harbor salvage group and the good folks at Puget Sound that had her ready for action in a little over two years. She sailed back to the Pacific on Independence Day, 1942.

Now for the real miracle. The U.S.S. *Oglala* was a minesweeper. At one time she was the pride of the Old Fall River Line. Long a New England legend, the Line operated between Fall River, Massachusetts, and New York City. She had also served in World War I. What she was doing as a member of the U.S. Navy's Pacific Fleet in December of 1941 is hard to fathom. She must have been part of one of the Navy's 1930's budget crunches.

For some reason or another she was a particular target of the

Japanese. Although badly damaged, she returned to the war in February of '44.

So, in the long run, what really did the Japanese gain from Pearl Harbor?

Of course, one can say they did get to be a super industrial giant. But as far as a big naval victory, in a few years the great Japanese Imperial Navy was to be at the bottom of the Pacific Ocean.

Richard Cheswick

◆

On December 7, 1941, I was a senior at South Side High School in Rockville Center, Long Island. I was in my bedroom doing Latin translations with one side of my head and listening to the New York Giants' football game with the other. They broke into the broadcast thusly:

"The Japanese have attacked the U.S. Naval Base at Pearl Harbor on the island of Oahu at Honolulu."

My God. I rushed downstairs where my parents were reading The *New York Times*. They couldn't believe it. I remember Dad asking me if I was sure. I told him I was. Dad had been a pilot in the First World War and was visibly shaken up, as was the whole country. I think you can safely say that everyone was in a state of complete shock.

At this point in time, the Germans were on the doorstep of Moscow. While Hitler did not declare war on us for a few days, I think everyone knew it was coming. To complicate matters, the early news from the Pacific was all bad. I remember saying to myself, "Hell, we can lose this war." I could visualize German and Japanese troops marching down the main street in Rockville Center, Long Island.

As for the attack on Hawaii, my reaction was absolute rage and it was many years before it changed. I can remember the newsreels of the Japanese diplomats in their morning suits and top hats, bowing all over the place. As I remember it, they were calling on

Cordell Hull at the very moment their planes were murdering our people at Hawaii.

This, of course, meant that America was now at war with the Axis Powers.

I did realize that this all must have been a tremendous blow to the very large isolationist and neutral groups in this country.

My parents were exactly the opposite. Our family was extremely pro Allies. They belonged to a group called Save America—Declare War Now. Naturally, this also made me quite pro Allies.

I spent the rest of Sunday constantly trying to get more news reports on what was going on. None of it seemed to be good.

So, the next morning, I asked my parents if I could join the Marines. You could get in the Navy or Marines at seventeen. Not the Army, you had to be eighteen there.

However, to join the Marines or the Navy, you had to get your parents to sign your enlistment papers.

Well, my parents knew I'd have to go, but they did have a suggestion.

"Dick," said Dad, "you'll be eighteen in July. Why don't you wait until your graduation and then we'll sign so you can join the Army Air Corps. There will be plenty of war left. But you must promise us you'll go to college when you get out." I agreed.

I must say, I don't think I got much out of that senior year. News of the war utterly dominated everything. I don't think the country will ever be united again the way we were the first years of the war. We can thank the bombing of Pearl Harbor for that.

Corporal Adam Rudalewicz, K-3—
27th U.S. Infantry

Sure I read the James Jones book *From Here to Eternity*. I think everyone who was in Pearl Harbor in those days has read it.

Did I enjoy it? You bet I did! Jones was in G Company in the 27th Infantry. It is a magnificent tale on what it was like to be in the Army in those days at Pearl Harbor.

For instance, did you want to make sergeant? Box, just like the book says. And if you could win your bouts, you could make first sergeant in a few weeks.

And it wasn't only boxing. We had all types of sports teams. We had baseball teams, basketball, football, everything you could imagine.

As for Fatso, there were guys like him everywhere. Each regiment had its own stockade. There was always a top sergeant in charge and many of them were real bastards. If you ended up in their hands, you could count on getting the hell kicked out of you at least once.

OK. Do you remember the officer's wife that Top Kick Warden was making out with? Well, Warden wasn't the only one getting someone's wife. Now, I'm not saying that they were all playing around, but some of those wives either weren't getting anything at home or they were a little weird.

We used to have what we called dog robbers, soldiers who were always sucking up to their officer. They'd mow their lawn, shine their shoes, clean up, and be generally useful.

This also meant they'd be in the officer's home, doing chores when the officer would be away in the field. Some could also manage to get into the officer's bed, if you know what I mean.

Then we had the woman who couldn't get enough. Here's an incident I can remember vividly.

I was on sabotage patrol one night in November of '41. We were in an area where many of the officers had their homes. We were supposed to be checking any civilians who were out after dark.

So, this woman is out walking. She seemed to be looking for something. I gave her the word.

"Ma'am," I said, "you really shouldn't be out this late. I'm on a sabotage patrol."

"Oh, Corporal," she answered, "I can't seem to find my cat. Have you seen him?"

"Well, not really, but if I come across a cat, I'll let you know."

"Oh, would you? I'd be ever so thankful. I live right here. That window with the light on is my bedroom. I'm home all alone. Just knock on my window if you find my cat. I'll be awake." Then she gave me a big smile and went home.

Well, hell, I don't even know if she had a cat, but she sure as hell was lonely. So, I waited about an hour and went and tapped on her window. She came over and opened the window.

"Hello, Corporal," she said, "did you find my cat? Come on in and tell me all about it."

Of course I went in. And when my relief came, I told him and he went in. Maybe his relief went in, too. She wasn't bad-looking either. I never went back though. I was playing with fire and I knew it.

Once again, let me make one thing straight. Most of the officers' wives weren't like that. But there were a few that couldn't get enough, if you know what I mean.

OK. I went into the Army from Dixon, PA, a small town of maybe five thousand people. There was no work around so in '37, I joined the C.C.C. I was sent to Aberdeen, Maryland, then out to Arizona. It was not a bad life. A bunch of young guys working outside all the time on public projects. We lived in camps somewhat like the Army. But when I got out in late '39, I had had enough.

Anyway, things still weren't going so good and with the war starting up in Europe, I figured what the hell, America had ended up over there back in '18; we'd probably eventually get into this one, too. Why not enlist in the Army?

So, I said to my mother: "Mom, why should I just hang around? I'm going to join the Army."

"Oh, Adam," she answered, "why do you want to do that? Don't you like your home?"

"Of course, but that thing going on in Europe isn't going away. We're going to get into it as sure as anything. This way I'll have lots of training. It might help me get home when it's all over."

That was it. A cousin of mine, also in Dixon, felt the same way. He joined up with me. We wanted to get into the artillery, but it wasn't to be.

We ended up on a transport called *The Republic*, headed for the Pacific. When someone told me we were going to Pearl Harbor, I was dumbfounded.

"Where the hell is Pearl Harbor?" I asked. I'd heard of it, but I didn't know where it was. I found out soon enough.

There was one thing that happened on *The Republic* that I'll never forget. I was standing on deck when the weather turned foul. I decided to go below so I could go to the head.

Wow, everybody is puking all over the place. You know how it is when you feel a little queasy yourself and you smell what everyone else is doing. I let loose and kept heaving. It was the only time in my life that happened to me.

Now, for Pearl. After we landed, we found out that my cousin was going into the 35th U.S. Infantry and I was slated for K Company, 3rd Battalion of the 27th Infantry. We were now both part of the 25th Division. It was strictly regular Army and I mean old regular Army.

In those days there was no special training for the Infantry.
You went through your basic training where you were going to
be stationed and they made it real chicken shit.

Hell, you could hardly speak to the real soldiers unless spoken
to. The rookies got every shit detail that came around, scrub the
barracks, polish the brass, clean out the latrine. It wasn't much
fun.

Well, one day I was polishing the brass when I got a little salty.
This sergeant named Gayieta was always called "Go Get 'Em" by
the regulars.

So, the sergeant gives me the word. "Chicken," (he always
called me chicken), "polish the brass over on the other side. Go
to it."

As it turned out, I was all out of polish so I spoke up.

"Jeez, Go Get 'Em, I'm all out of polish."

Christ, I thought the sergeant was going to explode. He roared
like a bull.

"It's *Sergeant* Gayieta to you, chicken. Go get some more polish and on the double!" I took off like that big-ass bird they were
always talking about, came back with the new polish, and went
to work. A little later I heard a roar. "Chicken, come here!" I
stood up as straight as I could and answered.

"That's *Private Rudalewicz*, Sergeant!"

Holy Christ! He is now about to really explode!

"Two weeks KP for you, chicken!" And that was that.

It's funny now, but it wasn't then. We weren't even second-
class citizens. We were at the bottom of the barrel. We couldn't
go to the movies or drink beer at the PX. But it finally ended.
Once we were really part of the regiment, everything went
smoothly. As a matter of fact I learned how to soldier with the
best of them.

For instance, every night around midnight a corporal would
come by and tie a KP sticker on each soldier's cot who was down
for KP the next day.

This night, around 0200, a soldier who was slated for KP came by and stuck his KP sticker at the foot of my bunk. I recognized him and an hour or so later I got up and stuck it back on his sack. I never heard a word about it. I guess that's what we called the old Army game.

By and large though, most everything went smoothly. I was soon made corporal and put in charge of a .60mm mortar squad, an essential part of a rifle company.

This was great, but standing over me I had this problem with my name. Boy, how this got butchered! The Army tried to insist my last name was Rudolph and most of my buddies started calling me Rudy.

What a mess! Someone told me that when U.S. Grant entered West Point, they changed his first name from Hiram to Ulysses. Hell, he died U.S. Grant. They never corrected the mistake.

Anyway, after the war I went to court to make sure everything that was official had the name Rudalewicz on it, not Rudy or Rudolph. The judge was befuddled.

"Young man," he said, "everyone else wants to shorten his name. How is it that you want to lengthen yours?"

"Simple, because Rudalewicz is my name, not Rudolph, Judge. This has been going on for six years. Do you know how hard it is to get the Army to change something like this?"

"Yes, young man, I do. But not anymore, Mr. Rudalewicz. No more Rudolph from here on in." That was it.

OK. Back to Pearl. It was around the first of October in '41 when they issued us gas masks, live ammunition, all that stuff. We had our .60mm mortars and the shells. We were more prepared for battle than at any other time while I was on Oahu. We were sent over to our battle positions at Fort Kam, right near the entrance to Pearl.

Then all of a sudden they sent us back to Schofield Barracks, some thirty miles from Pearl.

We all thought this was silly, but it seems maybe the Army and Army Air Corps had gone through similar exercises. Someone said they had lost the whereabouts of the Japanese task force, but they sure as hell hadn't found it by the first of December, or else they would have known it was heading toward Honolulu.

Anyway, we were back at Schofield and for that week I had a real cushy job. I had a jeep with a .30 caliber machine gun on the back. There were six of us in the vehicle. Our job was to drive all over the island, including the beaches, looking for sabotagers. And that's what I was doing on Saturday night, December 6, through the daylight hours of the seventh.

When we got to Schofield, it was time for breakfast. It was usually the same, eggs or waffles. Well, the morning of the seventh I didn't feel like either one. So I'd gone into the mess hall, sat down, and was having a cup of coffee.

Now, don't let me forget a guy in my outfit named DePree. The night of the sixth another soldier had gone up to DePree.

"Come on, DePree," he said, "lend me a few bucks. I'll pay you next week. I want to drink a few beers."

"Like hell," replied DePree, "we're going to war with the Nips tomorrow!"

Now, how in the hell did DePree know this? He was no genius, but he was right on target on that one. The soldier didn't get the money. When DePree saw the guy the next day, he just laughed. "I told you we'd be at war today. Haw! Haw!"

How right he was!

OK. As I said, it was time for breakfast. I was sitting in the mess hall. The first bomb that I heard came down. It sounded like it had hit near Wheeler Field.

"Wow," the guy sitting next to me said, "they must be having one hell of a training exercise! That sounded like a real bomb and it landed close."

So, we looked out the window. We could see all these planes buzzing around.

"Oh, Christ," another soldier said. "Look how low they're flying. They could crash into our mess hall, those jerks."

Then someone lets out a roar. "Those are real bullets those

bastards are firing. Look at those meatballs! The Japanese are attacking us. We're at war!"

I walked back into the kitchen, got some cereal, cream and sugar, came back, and was about to eat my breakfast. Then it hit me.

"Holy Christ, we're at war!" I yelled. But I didn't know what to do. I couldn't see what good mortar shells could do against planes.

I ran outside and I saw these soldiers from the 27th up on the roof firing rifles, BARs, and .30 caliber machine guns at the Japanese. I don't know how they expected to hit anything, but I do know at least one plane was shot down. I saw it the next day.

Anyway, it's now our job to get down near Fort Kam next to Pearl Harbor. I can remember that there was a lighthouse near the entrance to Pearl Harbor. That's where we belonged. We had to get there as soon as possible.

But many of our trucks had been taken for ambulances. We hadn't been hurt that badly, but Hickam Field had been clobbered.

Well, we finally got going. To reach our battle position we had to go by Hickam Field.

Christ, what a mess it was! I saw one sight I'll never forget. There was a soldier sitting in a jeep with no head. He was slumped over with his hands still on the wheel. I'll bet a lot of other guys from the 27th who saw the body in the jeep can remember it. There were other bodies lying all over the place.

Anyway, the Japanese left, but confusion was still everywhere. Let's go back to *From Here to Eternity*. You remember the scene where the soldiers are setting up their defense? That's what it was like. We were sure the Japanese were now going to invade Oahu.

I can recall one guy who was sure they'd attack.

"Look," he said, "if they'd wanted to set our oil supplies on fire, we couldn't have stopped them.

"Why didn't they? Because they hope to capture it. The Japs are really hard up for oil."

At least he did make some sense. Anyway, my squad was all

set up with our mortars. I'd look out to sea and wonder how many men the Japanese would send against us.

Of course I was worried about the outcome. The States were a long way away. But then somebody said something about how far they were from Japan.

Well, we never found out. They hauled ass back to Japan and never again attacked Hawaii.

Our outfit eventually went to Guadalcanal for tough service and later on to New Georgia. I was badly hurt near Buna and was sent back to the States. It was the end of the war for me.

And today, half a century since the attack, I look back on Pearl Harbor and do you know what I mostly think? What good duty that island was! That's what I think of.

Sneak or Surprise Attack?

◆

It is now fifty years since the day that will live in infamy had its hour in history. To the Japanese it was merely a surprise attack, an ambush, if you will.

During those fifty years the ultra nationalistic empire of Japan has gone through a complete change that is mind-boggling.

When Cordell Hull asked to have Kichisaburo Nomura shown into his office on December 7, 1941, it was 1:45 in the afternoon. Like so many other events of December 7 there is disagreement on the precise time.

However, what is fact is that Hull had just heard about the attack when Nomura entered his office. A shocked Hull lit into the startled Nomura. His denouncement ended with: ". . . infamous falsehoods and distortions on a scale so huge that I never imagined until today that any government on this planet was capable of uttering them."

Mr. Hull, that was a little heavy. Remember, just five months before, Hitler had instigated an attack on a quasially (the Soviet Union) who didn't have the slightest idea the Nazis were coming.

Would not Hull's words have been more appropriate if he could say today that no government on this planet has gone from the absolute bottom of the barrel to such a position of dominance?

Anyway, today Japan never uses the phrase "sneak attack." It is very apt to put the blame for the war on the United States, period.

No matter, the success of the attack was almost completely due to the American military not having the foggiest idea it was coming.

As it turned out, the majority of the damage done to the American fleet was accomplished by the first wave, while most of the damage done to the attackers was accomplished by an alerted antiaircraft defense during the second attack.

During the first attack the Americans brought down some nine planes while twenty planes were lost from the second wave.

What does all this mean? Visualize a Pearl Harbor that had been fully alerted in time to put all its planes (and they had over two hundred) in the air to greet the Japanese. Draw your own conclusion.

Well, one thing is a certainty. What has happened to Japan after she paid a horrible price for the attack is hard to realize.

So, sneak or surprise, it doesn't affect Japan today one way or another. It is no longer a nation in the tight grip of the military that goes around beating up its weaker neighbors. It is an extremely powerful industrial giant that does not know its strength.

But as for terms, to the American servicemen who were at Pearl, it will always be a sneak attack.

The Japanese Blast Ewa

◆

After the Pearl Harbor attack, a Japanese aviator wrote:
"I was diving down to take another run at Ewa. We had
already bombed the hell out of the place. I saw this one
American, standing next to a disabled plane. He just stood
there, firing and reloading his pistol. He didn't give an inch.
He was truly a Yankee samurai."

The airfield at Ewa was the largest Marine Air Corps base in the Pacific. It was really blasted by the Japanese on December 7.

During 1941 the airfield was greatly expanded. It was from here that the Marine planes were taken to Midway and Wake by the *Lexington* and the *Enterprise* a week or so before the raid.

The best of the lot was the squadron of twelve Grummans Major Paul Putnam, USMC, flew from the *Enterprise* to Pearl on December 4. Unfortunately, seven of these top planes were blown up by the Japanese. The remaining Grummans did a hell of a job before going down.

Well, when the Japanese did strike at Ewa, there was an assortment of some forty-eight planes lined up on the field. They were duck soup for the enemy. Forty-seven never even got off the ground. Let PFC Bob Wells, USMC, tell you what it was like.

Early Sunday morning I was on mess duty. My work assignment was in the spud locker. Two of us would prepare all the fresh vegetables for our Marine buddies at Ewa. That day we were slated to have sweet potatoes. We were working on them as fast as we could because when we finished, the mess sergeant would normally let us go on liberty.

So, we were peeling away when we noticed several airplanes flying very low. We figured it was either a Navy or Army drill.

Then I noticed these red balls on the wings. Our view was mainly blocked by the mess hall and the PX, but I knew something was wrong when this Marine officer came running by.

"Take cover, men," he said, "the Japanese are attacking us. We are now at war with Japan."

We didn't even have our rifles so we ran into one of the walk-in refrigerators, located behind the mess hall.

Wow, it was ten degrees in there. We quickly decided we'd rather be shot than freeze to death, so we ran out between the mess hall and the PX. Here we could see our airfield.

My God, what a sight! We had forty-eight planes of different types lined up. The Japanese planes had done a number on all of them.

The two of us each picked up bolt-action Springfield rifles. A jeep drove by with loaded bandoleers in it. A sergeant in the jeep was tossing out these bandoleers. We each caught one and went over to where they were building a new swimming pool. There was a bulldozer parked at the site. Using it for cover, we started shooting our rifles at the Japanese planes as they flew by. I don't think we hit anything, but we could let off some steam.

Then, out of nowhere, two American planes appeared. I later found out they were piloted by two Army men named Welch and Taylor.

Boy, did they tear into those Japanese planes! I saw two go down. There might have been more.

Well, after two waves had flown over, we were given the word.

"We have no more planes," we were told by an officer. "As of now, you are all Marine Corps riflemen again. The Japs may be coming ashore any minute now."

Well, as you know, the Japanese did not send troops ashore. Why, no one knew, but they surely knocked the American airfields to pieces. Not only Ewa, but also Wheeler, Bellows, and Hickam. Just about every place we had planes was devastated.

William Lehr, U.S.S. *Monaghan*

◆

My name is Bill Lehr. I went into the U.S. Navy from the state of Washington in August of 1940.

OK, you see my last name. Back at that time there was a dialect comedian named Lew Lehr. Do you remember him?

(At this point the author gave a poor imitation of Lew Lehr: "Monkeys is ze craziest people.")

That's the guy and that's the reason I was called Lew Lehr for my entire cruise in the Navy.

So, if you lived in a West Coast state, you automatically ended up in San Diego when you joined the Navy. Boot camp wasn't bad, but I couldn't wait to get aboard ship. I ended up a passenger on the U.S.S. *Colorado* on my way to Pearl Harbor.

There I found out I was to be in the dungaree navy, aboard the U.S.S. *Monaghan*. We were moored in a nest with three other tin cans, the *Farragut*, the *Dale*, and the *Aylwin*. Our skipper was a lieutenant named Bill Burford. Like most of the ships at Pearl, we spent our time going in and out of the harbor.

Well, a month or so before the attack, we had gone out on a patrol with the other destroyers in our nest. For the first time since I had joined the *Monaghan*, we practiced night patrolling. No lights topside and the smoking light was definitely not lit. We were to have nothing showing that would give the enemy a target. Our officers had heard the Japanese were experts at night fighting and they wanted us to practice after-dark maneuvers. During this exercise our officers and the top brass seemed to be getting quite serious about the situation with Japan.

And how did I know this? My battle station was at the wheel. I could hear what was going on and what our captain was saying to the *Enterprise* and the other ships in our group.

When we went out, it was almost always with the *Enterprise*. I can't remember why we didn't go with the Big E when it took some planes to Wake Island the first part of December, but, thank God, they missed out on the December 7 attack. The *Enterprise* was damaged several times during the war, but she was still afloat when the Japanese surrendered.

Among ourselves there was constant scuttlebutt about a possible war with Japan, but it lasted so long it got to be a joke with us. After all, way out in the Pacific like we were, if we had a war, it would have to be with Japan.

Well, some five weeks or so before December 7, we received a new order. We were told it was from Washington. All the ammunition was to be on the ready lockers at all times. We were to be on an alert twenty-four hours a day.

Then, two weeks later we got another letter from Washington. We were to put all the ammunition back down in the magazine. We were to go off full alert. Naturally we felt the crisis was over.

What happened then was when the attack did come, all our ammunition was down below in the magazine. The key to the magazine was in the captain's cabin.

Now, I ask you, the brass in Washington had to know how hot things were getting with Japan. What possible sense did it make to lock up all our ammunition just about as far away from the guns as was possible.

Of course, we all had heard the scuttlebutt about FDR wanting Japan to make the first move. Well, so what! They could have made the first move and we still could have had our ammunition on the ready lockers. You can bet your bottom dollars if that ammo was close by, we would have had a better shot at the Japanese during their first wave.

Here's another thing for you to ponder.

Sometime in the thirties an admiral decided he would sneak up on Pearl with a small task force just to show how easy it would be to pull a surprise attack on the Harbor.

They did this, taking the same northern approach the Japanese did in 1941. We heard the admiral didn't let the powers-that-be know he was there until he was about a hundred miles off Oahu.

The admiral's carriers' being that close to Pearl Harbor was a complete surprise to the powers-that-be at Honolulu. The admiral had done this just to show Washington that Pearl Harbor was highly vulnerable. The pity is no one paid any attention to him.

I did hear that Admiral King did not want our carriers ever to be caught at Pearl. And as it turned out, none of them were there on December 7, 1941.

The *Enterprise* had taken Grumman Wildcats to Wake and the *Lexington* was headed to Midway on maneuvers. The *Saratoga* was back on the West Coast for repairs. So, the Japanese came up with a big zero as far as their main targets were concerned.

Most of us believed the Japanese were completely fooled by the *Utah*. Once a battleship, this ancient relic had been turned into a target and supply ship. It had just returned from the West Coast with a large cargo of lumber. With all that lumber stretched out all over the Utah, it could have looked like a flattop from the air. Maybe that's why the Japanese took so much time and effort to put it on the bottom.

Well, on the night of December 6 we were outboard in our nest. That meant we were the duty destroyer of the four. So, the minute we saw the first planes, we knew we had to get under way as soon as possible. All hands immediately headed for their battle stations.

As I looked out, I saw a sight I'll never forget. Those planes were flying so low Dizzy Dean could have hit one with a baseball. One of those Japanese pilots actually smiled and waved at me.

Well, as quickly as we could, we got under way and headed for the exit from the Harbor. We had our full crew aboard and were aching for action. We were either the first or second ship at Pearl to get going. There seems to be a big disagreement here, but really, what difference does it make?

On our way out one of our eagle-eyed lookouts spotted something.

"Hey," he yelled, "look over there. Isn't that a periscope on our port side?" Sure enough, it was.

Just at that instant the Japanese sub fired a torpedo at us. The torpedo came to the surface, just bouncing along. Hell, we could see it plain as day. Thank God, it missed us. It went on over to the beach and exploded.

By this time we all figured it was one of those two-man subs the Japanese had. How in the devil could it have gotten into Pearl Harbor? Who knows? It was there. We were headed straight for it. The skipper wanted to ram the damn thing. And we did.

Wham! We cut the damn thing in two. And we stopped right on top of it.

At this point the executive officer grabbed a second-class torpedo man. The sailor had already dropped two depth charges on the sub.

"OK," the exec said, "drop two more."

"Oh, we can't do that, sir. You saw how the power from the first two lifted our bow out of the water. Besides, we've already cut the thing in two."

"Do as I say!"

"Sorry, sir."

"You're on report for rank insubordination!"

That was it. But I never heard any more about it. I'm sure the exec never pressed charges. He knew the torpedo man was right. Besides, the sub was cut in two anyway.

Well, we headed out to sea where we were soon joined by the three other tin cans in our nest. We lined up eight miles apart and started to scan the ocean. We kept getting our instructions from somewhere, but after a day or two we realized the guy had us headed back to the States.

After we were back in Pearl, we could find no record of who was giving us our directions when we were out to sea.

Apparently it was a saboteur in a shack up in the hills who could speak perfect English. Somehow he could cut into our frequency. He knew just what to say.

As for the two-man sub, the two pieces had been lifted up and deposited far out to sea. One of the dead Japanese was still aboard, but his head had been cut off.

Anyway, we found out that another destroyer, the U.S.S. *Ward*, had also sunk a two-man sub outside of the harbor about an hour before we did. Naturally, we felt badly about losing the distinction of sinking the first Japanese ship in what we all now knew was going to be a long war.

However, we did have a great moment some six months later at the battle of Midway. After all, this was revenge for Pearl Harbor. The four Japanese carriers our planes sunk in that crucial battle, the *Hiryu*, the *Soryu*, the *Kaga*, and the *Akagi* had all been at Pearl. The four were truly the aces of Admiral Nagumo's hand. And when they went down, so did so many of Japan's best aviators. They could replace neither the carriers nor the pilots.

Two months after Midway, the U.S. Marines invaded Guadalcanal. Pearl Harbor had bought the Japanese six months of conquest. After that it was all downhill for them.

Dick Thill, U.S.S. *Ward*

Lew Lehr was not the only person who mentioned the sinking of the Japanese sub outside of the harbor an hour or so before the attack on December 7. The ship that accomplished this sinking was the U.S.S. *Ward*, another tin can. Through the Survivors I was able to locate one Richard J. Thill, a ship's cook, 3rd class, who was serving on the *Ward* on December 7. I asked him if he remembered the sinking.

Sure, I do. We were patrolling the area just outside the Pearl Harbor entrance. We were called to General Quarters that morning because the U.S.S. *Condor* had reported an unidentified submarine in the restricted area. We could not find anything so we secured from GQ.

By 0630, daylight had arrived and we did spot a conning tower on what was obviously a two-man Japanese sub. Our number one and number three guns immediately opened fire. Number three scored a direct hit and we dropped four depth charges. It was curtains for the sub.

Our skipper, Lt. Bill Outerbridge, immediately sent off a message to headquarters at Pearl Harbor, telling them that the *Ward* had spotted a two-man Japanese submarine in a restricted area and that the *Ward* had definitely sunk same. We were later told that the lieutenant's call caused quite a stir among the Navy personnel back at Pearl, but it wasn't considered important enough to put the fleet on alert. I do know that our ship was credited with firing the first shot of the Pacific war.

And war being what it is, the *Ward* was sunk off the Philippines exactly three years to the day after the Pearl Harbor attack.

All of a Sudden, We Were Different

◆

Richard Erica was born on a small island off Portland, Maine, and, like so many natives of that magnificent state, still lives there.

"I went all over the world during my years in the Navy; never found a place I liked any better," said Richard.

He went into the Navy in August of 1940. At the end of the year he was sent to join the U.S.S. *Case* and he was aboard her at Pearl when the Japanese attacked Oahu. His memory of the prewar Navy is excellent. What he likes most is telling you how differently enlisted sailors were treated after the Pearl Harbor attack compared to how it was before December 7.

I remember sailing into San Francisco before the war started. If you didn't have bars on your shoulders, most decent places didn't want your money, what you had of it, anyway. But it was just as bad at Pearl. Here's what I mean.

In the summer of '41 I had gone to submarine school at the Navy yard. You know, I just wanted to get a feel of submarines.

So, this guy shows up at the Navy yard, wants to know if any of us are interested in taking any courses at the University of Hawaii. I certainly was.

"There is one stipulation," he added. "No one can show up with his uniform on. A lot of our students are antimilitary and we don't want any trouble."

Well, the hell with that! Somehow I had got the crazy notion we were protecting those islands from the Japanese. I said no thanks. That was the end of it.

After checking the landing rumors north of Oahu, we all headed south, looking for the Japanese.

Wow! As I look back, how lucky we were we didn't find them. We would have been outgunned tremendously.

Well, we came back to Pearl and I had a good look-see at what had happened to the Harbor. The Japanese had done a great job, but they could have done a lot more.

All the services: the Army, the Navy, and the Marines thought the Japanese would be following up the air attack with a landing. Here's my reasoning on why I didn't think so.

You see, there were God knows how many gallons of oil and gasoline all over Pearl. But neither the first or second attack waves of planes tried to start any fires. Surely they knew where we were keeping that oil.

Anyway, most of the damage to the fleet was done by the first wave. If those bastards in the second wave had gone after our fuel supply, they could have torched the whole island. That would have been the time to invade, but, thank God, they messed up on that one.

Then, a short time after December 7, we helped escort three damaged battlewagons to Bremerton, Washington.

Oh, my goodness, what a change! It was amazing. Everyone wanted to buy you a drink.

And the girls, you had to fight them off. All of a sudden we were all heroes. It was amazing what a difference a few bombs and torpedoes could make!

Robert Carmichael

Mr. Carmichael was born and bred in Texas. He served as a flier in the Naval Air Corps during World War II. He was awarded the Navy Cross for his actions in the battle for Leyte Gulf. Here is his reaction to the bombing of Pearl Harbor.

During the first week in December of '41 I was working near the Naval Air Station in Corpus Christi, Texas. I used to watch those pilots, just a year older than I, driving by in their convertibles. They usually had a good-looking young lady in tow. I knew that was where I was going to enlist if we got into the war.

You see, I was about halfway through the University of Texas over at Austin. I'd dropped out of school for a semester or two to get enough money to finish my education.

Well, I'd been out kicking the going around on Saturday night, the sixth of December. I was sleeping in.

Around noon I heard a vicious knocking on my door.

"Hey, Bob," someone yelled, "it's war. The Japs have bombed our base at Pearl Harbor." Of course I was pissed off at the Japanese in general. But above all I kept saying to myself what f___ idiots they must be.

OK. I wasn't surprised at the sneak attack. Living near Corpus Christi, I had kept up on American-Japanese relations. I knew they were close to the breaking point.

But for them to get all the way to Oahu and catch us with our pants down. What the hell happened?

Well, as you know, I did eventually get a chance to fly against dozens of Japanese planes. I am one guy who had a chance to avenge Pearl Harbor. I did the best job I could.

Vern Hirsch and Joe Carson

◈

Of the eight battleships at Pearl Harbor it seems that the *Tennessee* and the *Maryland* were the lucky ones. The *Tennessee* suffered five dead and the *Maryland* lost three crewmen.

Of course this is devastatingly tragic for those eight men and their families. But it pales next to the *Arizona*'s eleven hundred plus dead and the *Oklahoma*'s five hundred plus fatalities.

As one-sided as these figures may be, they do not mean that the *Arizona* and the *Oklahoma* were defended any less heroically or competently than the *Tennessee* or the *Maryland*. The whole thing depended on the luck of the draw.

Anyway, I had the good fortune to run into Vern Hirsch and Joe Carson while attending a meeting of the Pearl Harbor Survivors at Oceanside, California. Vern went into the Navy from Omaha, Nebraska, and Joe went in from Cleveland, Ohio. It was a most informative and pleasant sit-down.

Hirsch—I graduated from high school in 1936. That was the year FDR and Jack Garner thoroughly trounced Alf Landon and Frank Knox in the presidential election. Four years earlier FDR had promised to bring back prosperity. If he did, good times forgot to stop in Nebraska. That's where I lived and you didn't need a high school diploma to get a good job there then; you needed a magic wand.

So, I went over to Omaha and enlisted in the Navy. A week or two after I joined up, I was aboard a train headed for San Diego.

All right. Can you believe this? It took five days for that train to get to San Diego. So much for the old Rock Island Line. That ride in the middle of August was hell. Remember, there was no air-conditioning in those days.

Well, after boot camp I was ordered to report to the U.S.S. *Tennessee*. Our battleships were considered the pride of the fleet in those days. I was proud as a peacock.

Now, let me see. When did they move all those battlewagons to Pearl Harbor?

(At this point Joe Carson, also a Pearl Harbor veteran on the *Tennessee* joined us. Hirsch asked for confirmation.)

When did they move the *Tennessee* to Pearl Harbor, Joe?

Carson—April of 1940, I believe. But you know, I believe most of our shipmates were sick of Honolulu when the attack came. I know I was.

Hirsch—So was I. That's why we jumped at the chance on December 6 to see a football game between the University of Hawaii and Willamette University of Oregon. Joe and I were hoping Willamette would kick the bejesus out of Hawaii.

Carson—You can say that again! But by the time we had polished off all the beer we'd brought with us, I didn't think we cared a damn one way or the other.

Hirsch—Especially that fellow who came with us. I can't remember his name, but he had been on the *Tennessee* up until the middle of November. I think he had been transferred to a tin can.

Carson—Maybe so, but I am sure about one thing. He had a real beer jag on after the game. We didn't know what the hell to do with him.

Hirsch—And remember, he was a bosun first class. He was no boot.

Well, I was master-at-arms on the *Tennessee*. What the hell, I figured we'd take him aboard the *Tennessee* and let him sleep it off. So, we headed back to our ship around 0200 hours. We deposited our friend in the brig and hit the sack.

Carson—You know we weren't feeling any pain ourselves but our former shipmate was really inebriated.

Hirsch—Anyway, the next morning I figured I'd better go down below and send our sleeping beauty on his way.

Jeez, all of a sudden I heard all this noise. Then the loudspeaker came through.

"This is no shit. Get your butt to your battle station. The Japs are attacking Pearl Harbor. I repeat, this is no shit. Get a move on!"

Next the bugler came on. We couldn't tell what the hell he was blowing. Then he went into the cavalry charge and kept blowing it. I figured, the hell with our friend in the brig. He was going to be as safe there as anywhere. I went to the quarterdeck to see what was going on.

At this point the first bomb landed on turret number three. It killed a CPO and two others.

Carson—My God, what confusion! None of us had been under fire before. We'd practiced what to do for years and we were doing it. But this was by rote. I don't think most of us really gave it a thought. We just did it.

Then came the second bomb. It split the gun on turret two. I think we lost two more men there.

The thing that stands out foremost in my memory is the confusion that followed that second bomb. Everyone was still doing his job but we were saying things like, "Why are those creeping bastards doing this to us?"

Hirsch—After the second bomb we could look over and see the *West Virginia* was taking a hell of a beating. It looked as if it might go over on its side. It was outboard and had squeezed us in. We could see the *Oklahoma* was already over on its side.

Carson—That second bomb threw out shrapnel all over the place. Some of it ripped out the stomach of Mervyn Bennion, the skipper of the *West Virginia*. A doctor got to him in a hurry, but it was too late. He was soon a goner.

At the same time the *Arizona* exploded. Christ, they could have heard that noise back in California! The force of that tremendous blast did more damage to the *Tennessee* than the two bombs that hit the ship put together.

Hirsch—One of our ship's major problems was the flames from the *Arizona*. The fires were blazing away at full tilt. And all the oil that was oozing out of the *Arizona* was a real threat.

Carson—Well, somehow a blaze had reached back into officers' country. The captain's quarters caught fire and there was hell to pay. Remember, the bow of the blazing *Arizona* was a mere sixty yards or so from the *Tennessee*. We were afraid that fire would get below decks. That would have meant real trouble.

Hirsch—My battle station was at the broadside battery. We couldn't use that gun. As I looked over, the *Weevie* (nickname for the *West Virginia*) seemed to be leaning over drastically. Thank God it never went over like the *Oklahoma*.

So, I decided to help haul ammunition up from below for our five-inchers. Oh, hell, it seemed like everyone and his brother was doing that. A chief told me and one other guy to get a fire hose to help keep the oil fires from spreading. We got the hose and did our best. But it was no fun. While there were no more bombs falling on us, we were constantly being strafed.

Now here's one for you. When the Japanese planes would get close, we could see their machine-gun bullets getting nearer and nearer. We'd jump under this canvas covering.

After we did this twice, my partner in crime started to laugh. He held up the canvas.

"What a couple of assholes we are!" he said. "This couldn't stop a BB gun. What the hell are we, ostriches? We may not be able to see them under this canvas, but they sure as shit can shoot us dead!"

We both had a good laugh. The next time they came over we just kept pumping water.

Carson—OK, Henry, you showed us a picture in that presentation you put on. The one that had the *Tennessee* and the *West Virginia* in it. You could plainly see our hoses going full tilt on the fantail. Our big fear was those oil flames from the water engulfing our ship.

Anyway, our captain was a real smart cookie. He had our props going all night long. Of course we weren't going anywhere but that could help keep the oil fires from coming aboard. He also turned the screws over. Whatever he did we kept the fires out.

Hirsch—Yes, we were still pinned against the keys. We had to use dynamite on those keys to get out later on.

We did get out to sea rather quickly though compared to the other battleships. I think it was about the sixteenth of December. We were under way about two days when our skipper, Charley Reordan, called us to General Quarters.

"Men," he said, "I have a Christmas present for you. We're heading for Bremerton, Washington, for repairs and should be there in time for Christmas."

This surely was good news. Basically, the old man was pretty popular. I was told he had a Panama hat on during the battle, but I didn't see him.

Carson—They surely worked on us at Bremerton. After that we went down to San Francisco for some more work. They were working like hell to get us back in the war. When they figured we were seaworthy, they sent us up near the Aleutians as part of the Navy's feint at the time of the Midway battle. After that I left the *Tennessee*.

There's one more thing I'd like to tell you. Two weeks or so before December 7 a group of us were transferred to the *West Virginia* for what turned out to be the last peacetime patrol we had. I think the *Oklahoma* also came out on the quick cruise. It seems we were always shorthanded. I was to go back to the *Tennessee* after the patrol.

As it turned out, they must have had secret orders in the safe because on the way back we went on a zigzag course.

That was something new to me. I tried to find out why the captain did that, but nobody knew. I'm not trying to make a big deal out of it, but the captain must have known more about the situation with Japan than we did.

Hirsch—Well, I left the *Tennessee* before Joe did. I picked up some shrapnel in my leg from that bomb that hit us on turret two. I tried treating it myself mainly because I didn't want to get stuck in the Naval Hospital at Honolulu. But by the time we got to the States I had to turn into sick bay. Besides, a little free time in San Francisco was very appealing.

OK, as Joe has told you, the *Tennessee* was back in action in '42. We were luckier than some of the other battleships.

But I never did hear what happened to that other sailor we were drinking beer with at the football game. I do know that where he was sleeping it off was not damaged by the Japanese. However, I just don't know if he got into any trouble or not.

Lou Trantales, Machinist 2nd Class,
U.S.S. *Pennsylvania*

◇

I went into the Navy in 1940. It wasn't very long after I enlisted that I became a machinist's mate aboard the U.S.S. *Pennsylvania* at Pearl Harbor. This was the flagship of the Pacific Fleet.

As a matter of fact I can remember when Admiral Kimmel took over his command from another admiral named Richardson. That was sometime in early 1941.

So, on December 6 we had just come off patrol in the Pacific. We had moved into Dry Dock Number One. There were two destroyers with us. They were the *Downes* and the *Cassin*. They were keeping dangerous company. I don't think the Japanese were after destroyers. But in going after the *Pennsylvania*, the enemy also blasted the two destroyers to kingdom come.

We later heard that Fuchida, the leader of the Japanese fliers, was quite disappointed when he found out that we were in dry dock. He had wanted personally to put a torpedo into the *Pennsylvania*; tough thing to do if a ship is in dry dock.

Whatever, around dawn on Sunday morning I went ashore to go to Sunday school. They had set up a place on the beach where each Sunday you could go and receive religious instructions. I guess this was to keep us from the evils of Hotel Street. After it was over they'd take us back to our ships in a motor launch.

Wow, as I got into the launch, the air was filled with Japanese planes. They were bombing and strafing everywhere, but they didn't strafe the launch.

When I got on board, someone was yelling, "General Quarters, this is no shit," over and over.

I went to my battle station, which was down below next to the magazine. There I stayed until long after the second wave had gone by. Each time we took a bomb hit we could feel the vibration.

Naturally our skipper, Captain Charles Cooke, felt as if he'd been trapped there in dry dock. We were told he was very upset when a five-hundred-pound bomb had torn his friend Lieutenant James Craig to bits.

And that's when I got the biggest shock of my life. It must have been close to noon when I finally got above deck and saw all those dead bodies. We had lost several men from the attack. Many of them were getting ready to go ashore for Sunday liberty when they were killed.

As I looked at all those corpses, a cold chill went up and down my spine. It must have been the main magazine that blew up on the *Arizona*. It was still covered with black smoke.

My God, what if a bomb had gotten through to where I had been during the attack? There wouldn't have been enough left of me to bury.

All right, I served in the Navy throughout the war. When I got back home to New Haven, I went into the restaurant business. Just sold my restaurant a short time ago after forty years.

I must be in pretty good shape though. In 1989 I joined a group supporting the American Lung Association. We all stuck our bicycles aboard a plane going to Seattle. Then we jumped aboard.

Next we cycled to Washington, D.C, some thirty-five hundred miles away. I was the only Pearl Harbor Survivor in the group. But we got this million dollars in donations for the American Lung Association. That's not chicken feed!

Cleaning Out the Hospital

Charley Hine was a Missouri farm boy. Charley went to St. Louis and became a cabdriver. He wanted to make enough money so he could get to college. He was earning about six dollars a week, which just about paid for his room and board. In other words he was on the well-known treadmill to oblivion. Tell it like it was, Charley.

Oh, that's right. I was getting nowhere so I figured I'd join the Navy. After boot camp in San Diego I went to the base hospital where I learned to be a corpsman. A year or so later I was assigned to the Naval Hospital at Hospital Point on the island of Oahu. I arrived there in January of '41.

OK. Now, as I think I've told you, I loved all sports. I played for the hospital team in basketball and baseball. I can remember our pulling off a big upset by beating the U.S.S. *California*'s basketball team.

Well, things were going great. I liked my work and was getting pretty good at it. This also meant I was advancing in rank.

Then came the morning of December 7. We had an excellent view of the attack. Occasionally some bombs would fall nearby.

Anyway, I watched the two waves go over and I didn't see a single Japanese plane get knocked down. It was later documented that we shot down twenty-nine Japanese planes, but I didn't see any of our planes in the air.

A Japanese plane did come down behind the hospital. I went over on Monday to look at it. Its spark plugs were spread all over the lot. They said right on them, "Champion Spark Plug—Toledo, Ohio." I wonder how much of their shrapnel also came from the U.S.?

Now, here's what I remember most about the raid. On Saturday night we had four hundred beds full at the hospital. By Monday, all but six of the original patients had gone back to their ships. And the six who were left had been operated on Friday or Saturday.

Oh, we were full again, and then some. But all our original patients wanted to get to their ships or posts. Everyone wanted a crack at those Japanese. Of course, it's quite possible some of our sailors didn't have to be there in the first place. There are always a few goldbricks around.

Sergeant Harold Slater,
64th Coast Artillery

As I have previously stated, there is no way I could have completed this book without the generous help I received from the Pearl Harbor Survivors Association.

During a two-year period I visited with this group from Maine to California. I would meet with two or three of these veterans and actually attend their meetings.

On July 23 of 1990 I attended a meeting of the Nutmeg Chapter of the Pearl Harbor Survivors. I had planned to interview one Harold Slater, formerly of the 64th Coast Artillery, U.S.A. Of course, we were interrupted by other members of the Survivors. These meetings are not too formal.

At the meetings I attended you have not only the survivors but their wives. The main idea behind these gatherings is to keep alive as long as possible what happened at Oahu in 1941 and to have a good time as they do this.

Now for Harold Slater of the 64th antiaircraft unit on Hawaiian shores.

Well, I was seventeen years of age in '39, working in a quarry in Glastonbury, across the river from Hartford. I had hoped to become a stone cutter. My dad was a foreman at the quarry. He came over to me one day.

"Harold, my boy," he said, "this place is going belly up. You'd better look around in a hurry."

That was enough for me. The next day I walked across the river (Connecticut) to Hartford and made the rounds, but it was no soap. The damn depression was still around, believe me. A company would be crazy to hire a kid like me when there were plenty of older men looking for work.

Anyway, I was kind of fed up with the area so I said to myself, "What the hell, why not join the Army?"

So, I was walking down the street in Hartford and I saw this sign proclaiming, "We Want You!" I looked at the sign and saluted.

"OK, buddy," I said, "you got me."

I walked in and was quickly greeted by an old-time sergeant with chevrons and hash marks up and down his sleeve. We talked for quite a while. He painted a pretty picture, especially when it came to the money. Twenty-one dollars a month wasn't much, all right, but remember all those extras. Plus, if you went overseas, you'd get extra dough. So I took the Queen's shilling, as they used to say.

The Army first asked me where I wanted to go.

"As far away from here as possible," I answered.

"OK," I was told, "we can send you to China, the Philippines, or Honolulu."

China sounded great to me. That was it. You see, I had a cousin in the Army in China. Perhaps I could tie up with him.

In those days you didn't take your basic training until you got to your permanent base. They surely didn't waste any time with me. In a week or so I was off.

We were about halfway to California when we got the word. We were all going to Honolulu. That also sounded great to me. Native girls doing hulas, Dorothy Lamour, all those beauties.

As I look back on it, I got a lucky break. Most of the men who went to China were either killed or captured later on by the Japanese. We had a lad from Glastonbury who went into the Army shortly before I did. He was captured. He did get back home but died a few years later. His life wasn't worth a hill of beans after eating all that Japanese prison crap.

Our ship landed in Oahu on December 13, 1939. Hawaii was considered foreign duty in those days so I could count on coming home on December 13, 1941. As a matter of fact the ship, the *Army of the Republic*, was sitting off Pearl Harbor on December 7, 1941. Most of my stuff was already aboard her. I don't know why the Japanese didn't hit her. I guess they had other fish to fry.

I ended up in an antiaircraft outfit, the 64th Coast Artillery. The duty was great. They made me a heights finder. My job was to find out how high up any attacking aircraft would be.

The 64th was quartered at Fort Shafter some eight miles from Pearl but our field position was at Salt Lake Crater, near the entrance to Pearl Harbor. They moved us over to the Crater in November of '41. We stayed there until the first of December in '41. We had our .90mm guns in position, loaded for bear. If we had been at the Crater on the seventh on full alert, we could have inflicted a lot of damage on those Japanese planes. I never found out why they moved us back to Shafter when they did. They told us we were to be in a big parade, but I don't remember one.

(At this point we were interrupted by the congenial John Grand Pre. John takes things in stride.)

"Do you fellows know the difference between a fairy tale and a sea story?"

(Neither of us did.)

"Then here it is. A fairy tale opens up like this: 'Once upon a time.' A sea story begins with 'This ain't no shit.' "

(We both laughed. Then Harold got back to his story.)

For the next year or so after I landed at Oahu I went to stereoscopic school to learn my trade. It seems I had the knack of finding out how high up a plane was at any time. They made me a sergeant. I tried to teach the other guys in my outfit what I had learned.

Now for the big day. On the first weekend in December I was

in charge of quarters. I am one soldier who was not on liberty on December 7.

A whole group of us were in our barracks getting ready for one of those great Sundays we had in the Army in those days.

All of a sudden we started hearing all these planes. Our barracks had a huge old-fashioned porch. We all ran out to see what was going on.

Then we heard the bombs and machine-gun fire at Hickam. We still didn't know what the hell was going on. It was weird.

Oh, I guess we thought if anyone was attacking us, it had to be the Japanese. One of our guys mentioned the Germans, but how the hell could they get to Honolulu?

Whatever, how we wished we hadn't left the entrance to Pearl Harbor a week earlier. We all felt we should go to our assigned area as soon as we could, but could we move that fast? We also had to get our ammunition out of the storeroom, but we couldn't find the guy with the key. Someone said they had seen him dead drunk over at Waikiki Beach. When we heard that, we simply got together and broke down the door.

In the meantime some Japanese noticed our outfit. They scored a bull's eye on E Battery's barracks. Oh, we knew who was bombing us now. I guess we always did.

Next, some planes started strafing all around us. It was the first time most of us had been under fire. The Japanese were talking to us loud and clear with their bullets. They were saying, "WAR! WAR! WAR!"

Next, I was put on traffic detail as we tried to move over to the Crater. At this time the order came down to fix bayonets. Jeez, did you ever try directing traffic while carrying a bayoneted rifle? I cut my hand quite badly and had to stop off at the hospital.

(At this time John Caputo joined us.)

John—"Did you get a Purple Heart?"

Harold—"No."

John—"Gee, Slater, I heard that they were giving everyone at the hospital a Heart. They even went through the gonorrhea ward hanging Purple Hearts on the patients' beds."

Can you imagine a little girl talking to her father? "Dad," she'd say, "how did you get your Purple Heart?"

Dad—"For getting the clap, dear. All in the line of duty."

(Back to Harold.)

That's right, Joe. I knew guys who got the Heart for falling over the barbed wire we had set up.

You see, we all felt the Japanese would be coming back for an invasion. Most of us were very concerned. How many would be coming? We were thoroughly confused. Some of our own PBYs came over and one disoriented officer was firing his .45 caliber pistol at them. I think the guy had flipped his lid.

(At this juncture, Harold broke out a photo album with pictures of celebrities who had visited Oahu in 1941.)

Look, here's Shirley Temple, Dorothy Lamour, and Sonja Heine. And here's Judy Canova. They say she got drunk and went to bed with an Army corporal. Don't know if it was true or not, but if so, hooray for Judy! Most of those celebrities were officers' stuff. But not this guy. He went over to Waikiki Beach and hit fungoes out into the ocean for hours. The kids were going crazy trying to get one. The man hitting the balls was named Babe Ruth.

Well, as for the attack, the old 64th didn't get a shot off. I stayed on Oahu until the spring of 1944. I had a great furlough and returned to duty down on Cape Cod. In the fall I went back overseas, this time to Europe. I ended up in the frozen ice land they called the Battle of the Bulge. There's something for you! From Waikiki Beach to Belgium in the dead of winter. Some difference!

However there is one thing above all that I'll always remember about December 7, 1941. The 64th's duty was to help protect Pearl Harbor. Why in hell's name didn't they leave us at the neck of Pearl Harbor? We were on full alert there. We could have done some real good there instead of not shooting down one plane, which is what happened.

Here and There: Take It Easy on Your First Cruise

◈

Herb Frank was a PBY gunner in a patrol squadron at Pearl Harbor in the fall of 1941. They had been ordered to greatly increase their patrolling in November, but they were never told how far to go out in the Pacific. Herb finally went over to this old salt Chief Petty Officer.

"Hey, Chief," asked Frank, "that is one hell of an ocean out there! How far out do we go?"

The chief smiled that patronizing smile the old-timers reserved for the young sailors.

"Young fellow," he answered, "turn back when you see your first Japanese fishing boat."

It took a while before Frank realized the chief was putting him on.

An Underrated Man

William Franklin Knox was secretary of the Navy on December 7, 1941. A Republican, Mr. Knox was strictly a political appointee. Roosevelt knew war was coming and he wanted as nonpartisan a Cabinet as he could get. The publisher of the *Chicago Daily News*, Frank, as he was called, had been Alf Landon's running mate in '36.

Knox once said, "I am having fun playing-sailor."

And if the truth be known, the uniform brass didn't pay much attention to old Rough Rider Knox. But the letter he sent Cordell Hull a week before the Japanese attack on Pearl proves he was no clown.

It said, "It looks very much like we're going to war with Japan quite soon. It will probably start with a surprise attack at Pearl Harbor."

For that letter alone Mr. Knox should have received great accolades from his government. Too bad Cordell Hull paid no attention to it.

On the Beach

There were four types of women at Oahu. First the working ladies of Hotel Street. Then the so-called nice girls. Then men called them officers' stuff. When you saw them, you could easily see their parents had big bucks.

Number three would be the legitimate working women, the kind who wouldn't mind taking an enlisted man home to meet the family.

And finally, the ones who followed the fleet. They'd show up when the big ships would come in.

They had great names like Battleship Betty, Salty Susie, Hefty Helen, and the likes.

Most of them had been married to sailors and many of them more than once. Others had current husbands or lovers who were out to sea.

So, one veteran, who didn't care to be identified, told me of meeting such a beauty at Waikiki Beach.

"Oh, she was a beaut, all right," he told me. "She had the word 'sailors' tattooed on the inside of one thigh and 'entrance' on the inside of the other one."

December 6, 1941

"Today is the day that the Japanese are going to bring their answer to Cordell Hull and everything we have indicates they have been keeping the answer until the right time in order to accomplish what they want to. Something is hanging in the air. No doubt about it."

> —From the diary of
> COLONEL HENRY L. STIMSON,
> Secretary of War

Dick Phelan

◇

On December 6, 1941, I turned seventeen and I was in love. Her name was Mildred. The sixth was also the date of her high school prom. We were living in the Bronx but the prom was at the Hotel Astor in Manhattan.

Wow, what a party! We ended up riding the Staten Island Ferry. It must have been around 6:00 A.M. when I got home. I hit the rack and slept like a baby.

Around 2:00 in the afternoon I hear my father's voice.

"Hey, kiddo, get your ass out of the rack. The Japs have bombed Pearl."

"Pearl what?" I answered.

"Pearl Harbor, it's our naval base in the Hawaiian Islands. It means war."

"OK, I'm ready, Dad. You're a former Marine. You've been telling me how great the Corps is. Now I'm going to find out."

"Good for you, son. I'm too old but I'll go down to the recruiting office with you tomorrow."

It was set. Then Mother found out.

"Don't be crazy. You're only seventeen. I'm putting my foot down. You're not going anywhere until you're at least eighteen."

That was it. Mother's word was law. I didn't go into the Corps until the first part of '43.

Well, like everybody else I was infuriated by the Japanese attack. Then I realized that two good friends of mine were going to suffer. They were Japanese-Americans. But to me they were just people.

You know, back in '41 the Bronx was made up of neighborhoods. As far as I was concerned my Nisei friends were just part of the old neighborhood. They had a hard time of it though after the Japanese attack.

Now, back to my girlfriend, Mildred. I went overseas and all the while I was out there I sent money home. When I got back, she had every cent stashed away in the bank for me. I got the money but not Mildred. She married a Coast Guardsman, who spent the entire war at Manhattan Beach. That's the way it goes.

Edward J. Gunger,
U.S. Army Air Corps

◆

I have nothing against today's kids. Hell, we raised nine of our own. But they do look at things differently than we did though.

Take two of my boys. They both went in the Marine Corps. They'd tell me some of the things they did and I'd just laugh.

"What the hell are you boys in, the Boy Scouts? You don't sound like the Marines I knew at Pearl. You could never get away with that stuff in the Marines in those days."

Another of my sons was in the Air Force, like his dad, only we called it the Army Air Corps in those days. We were all spit and polish, just like the Marines, but not my son's outfit. Things have changed. No doubt about it!

All right, let's go back to '38. I was nineteen. I was crazy about sports.

But I read the other parts of the paper also, particularly the international stuff. You didn't have to be a genius to realize that nut Hitler was a bad news egg. It seemed to me that another war was building up.

So, I decided to enlist in the Army Air Corps. I'd always been interested in flying. Even if we didn't go to war, I figured I could really learn something about flying to use in later life.

The next thing to do was to tell Dad I was going to join up. Oh, boy, he wanted no part of it.

"Son," he said, "maybe there'll be another war, maybe not. But you'd better wait and see. And that's final!"

225

That was it. Fifty years ago, you did what Dad wanted you to do and no ifs, ands, or buts. I got a job working for the Dictaphone Corporation and waited until I was twenty-one. Once again I faced Pop.

"Dad," I said, "I'm my own man now and I still want to join the Army Air Corps." Dad didn't say much, but I still don't think he liked it. The next day I went over to Bridgeport and enlisted and that was it.

As I look back now, I find it hard to believe that things happened as fast as they did. The Army needed men on active duty at that time and the first thing I knew I was a buck-ass private at Hickam Field on the island of Oahu. As we used to say, "It was good duty." There was, however, constant tension in the air.

You see, by this time Hitler had overrun most of Europe. Germany and Japan, and don't forget Mussolini, had a pact and were called the Axis Powers. If the U.S. went to war with Germany, Japan would undoubtedly join Hitler. We all knew how important Oahu would be if that happened.

But tension or no tension, life was pretty good. Most of the time I was doing aerial photography and handling the .50 caliber gun on a B-17.

And I'll tell you something, I definitely was not one of the men who couldn't wait to get off duty and go to some of the bars like the Black Cat, the Green Lantern, or Trader Vics, just to name a few. Hell, it seems they were everywhere. Not for me.

Then there was Hotel Street. That was just one big cathouse. As far as I could see, I think the bars and the brothels were the number one and number two money-grabbers from the servicemen at Pearl.

What I did was enroll in a night course at the University of Hawaii. I went there for about seven months before Tojo interrupted my education.

All right, by the middle of October in '41 things got real serious. We received an order signed by no one else but FDR. It ordered us to remain on twenty-four-hour alert until further notice.

Wow! Did they run our asses off! We had planes in the air twenty-four hours a day. I recall one day when I didn't close my eyes for at least twenty-four hours. A young lieutenant noticed me.

"All right, Gunger, you look beat," he said to me. "Go back to your quarters for four hours of sleep."

Hell, I thought to myself, can this clown spare me for four hours? Big deal!

Anyway, we were all told on Saturday afternoon, December 6 that the alert was off. We heaved a sigh of relief. We figured we all could get some rest.

Now, I cannot explain why, but after the second wave of planes had gone over, something told me to go to the bulletin board and see if the original order was still there. It was. I grabbed it and stuck it in my foot locker. I still had it when the war ended and I kept it for many years.

But, you know, we raised nine kids and somehow it disappeared. What I'd give to have it today!

Now for December 7. When I hit the hay on Saturday night, I was still beat from all that flying. I conked off right away and I mean I was really dead to the world.

I came to around 0730 or 0745 the next morning to the cursing of one of my buddies.

"What the hell are they doing? Having maneuvers and no one told us about it?" he's groaning.

I looked out the window and spotted the rising sun on the planes. They were flying so low you could see the faces of the pilots.

"Maneuvers, hell, those are meatballs!" I yelled.

That was it. My God, everyone is running around, bumping into each other. Someone yells, "Let's go to the arsenal!" So we started out the door. I think it was then Don Meagher got hit with something and was burned to a crisp. He was my crew chief. He was the first man I saw killed and it was very sobering.

We got to the arsenal and would you believe it? There's a sergeant there and he's yelling, "I can't unlock the door without a signed order."

Oh, man, did the boys give him the business! I think "horse's ass" was one of the milder things they called him.

Finally, everyone seemed to hit the door at the same time. Hell, we just knocked that door off its hinges. We all grabbed something and started firing.

By this time we could see what a tremendous job those Japanese had done on our planes.

All right, what I am going to tell you still haunts me to this day. I had a great buddy named Louie Sitzer. I could see two B-17s over on the other end of the field that hadn't been touched. I turned to Louie.

"Hey, Lou," I yelled, "see those two B-17s over on the other end of the field? Let's run over and see if we can shoot down some of those bastards."

We started off, then all of a sudden, Lou stopped and started firing a .45 at this low-flying plane.

"Lou," I yelled, "cut it out. You can't hit anything with that peashooter. You'll get killed!"

Oh, my God, just as I yelled, they hit him with something heavy that seemed to about take his head off. What was left of my good friend just collapsed. I sometimes still dream about Lou getting killed. It was horrible!

I made it to the planes and climbed in one of them. There was another airman already there. I helped him all I could to keep firing. I don't know if we hit anything or not, but at least we showed the Japanese we were there.

After the second wave had passed over, we looked around. What a mess! They had caught most of our planes on the ground. This was very important to their plan of attack. If we had been able to put a couple of hundred planes up in the air to meet them, we could have thrown a monkey wrench in their whole operation.

Well, we didn't. They caught us with our pants down and that's all there is to it.

Another thing I should tell you about is this old sergeant we had called Old Mac. Old, hell, he was probably forty-five or so. We called that old in those days.

Mac had gone into the Air Service during the first war. I don't know what actually was his job at Hickam Field. It seems every time I saw him he was drinking beer.

So, what did Mac do when the attack started? No one seemed to know because he was just not seen by anyone.

As it turned out, he snuck into this beer hall we had. If Mac was going to get killed, he wanted to go out happy.

Anyway, an hour or so after the attack someone says, "Hey, has anyone seen Sergeant Mac?" No one had. We started looking everywhere, fearing the worst.

There was another old soldier in our outfit who just snickered.

"Look," he said, "I've been soldiering with this guy for years. Has anyone looked in the beer hall?"

So, there he was, surrounded by empty beer cans with this shit-eating grin on his face.

"Did we knock the hell out of those Nips?" he asked.

The war got really serious after December 7 and I don't know if he survived it. But I do hope if that old soldier did get killed that he had a beer can in his hand when he went.

Another lighter moment concerned a Filipino civilian who worked at the airfield. I had noticed this little guy, sitting at a bus stop when the first wave was coming over.

He was still there after the second attack had finished. By this time he had had enough. He's yelling in broken English.

"Hey, where the hell is my bus? I'm hungry!"

But it wasn't all fun and games. However, when we realized what had happened, we sure needed a good laugh.

Our barracks were in shambles and God knows how many planes we had lost. And the men. We had all lost good buddies. This was very sad.

And if we looked across at Pearl Harbor, wow, we really knew we were at war and it wasn't going to be any snap.

Well, the next day there was all confusion and fear. We all felt sure the Japanese would be back and soon. We put up all the planes we could while our repair men were working as fast as possible, trying to fix the damage that had been done to many of the others.

I had first taken a plane up at about 1700 hours on the seventh and had kept going up for weeks.

We were all itching for a fight. I'd see plenty of action later on in the Pacific, but I don't think I would ever be as anxious for it as I was immediately after Pearl. I'd scan the sky through the turret, thinking of Louie and the other men we had lost on the seventh.

And, if not my friends, I'd be thinking about what would have happened if that all-alert order had not been canceled on December 6. We had 347 planes destroyed or damaged on December 7. If they had been on full alert, they could have shot the Japanese out of the sky.

Cunningham of the U.S.S. *Nevada*

All right. You asked me if I had any idea how close we were to war with Japan a few weeks before their raid on Pearl Harbor.

Yes, I think I did.

When we went out to sea the last week in November, we were given the word to sink any Japanese ships we ran into.

OK. I was raised in Arkansas. In the fall of 1940 they started the draft and were calling up the National Guard all over the country. I'd never seen an ocean in my life, but I somehow figured I'd be better off in the Navy than digging ditches in the Army. So, I figured I'd beat them to the punch. I joined the Navy.

My next stop was San Diego. After a short boot camp I found myself a passenger on the U.S.S. *Saratoga*, headed for the island of Oahu. There I became Seaman 2nd Class Dwight Cunningham on the U.S.S. *Nevada*. My rating would go up, but I would be on the *Nevada* for the next three years.

Well, let's get to December 6 of '41. On that day the *Nevada*'s crew spent most of the day taking ammunition off the ship. The *Pennsy* was in dry dock. We were slated to replace her when she came out. The only ammunition we could put our hands on when the Japanese did come was the ammo in the Ready Box. We needed more than that.

Anyway, I went ashore the night of December 6, had a few beers, and was back on board around 2300 hours. I was dead beat and hit the rack at once.

I wanted to get up early on Sunday morning because I was going to visit a pal from my hometown of Benton, Arkansas. He was serving aboard the U.S.S. *Tennessee*, another battlewagon. I think we were going to meet at the Black Cat, a bar across from the YMCA.

So, the next morning I hit the deck at around 0700. I showered, shaved, brushed my teeth, and put on a clean pair of whites. I looked pretty snappy if I do say so myself.

I was about to go topside when I heard a hell of a racket from over on Ford Island. I looked out a porthole and all I could see was black smoke. Then I saw a hangar explode. Something was up, no doubt about it!

I ran up the nearest ladder and got the biggest shock of my life. There were all these darn planes buzzing around like hornets. I had never seen anything like it. How in the hell they weren't bumping into each other I just don't know.

At roughly the same time our loudspeaker started blaring General Quarters over and over. My battle station was turret number one. I headed for it.

As I was on my way, I couldn't help but notice what great pilots those Japanese must have been. They were flying so low they were just clearing the midship mast.

Our captain was a man named Francis Scanland. He was spending the weekend ashore as was his executive officer. The senior man aboard was a lieutenant commander named Francis Thomas, one of the few Reserve officers we had. Mr. Thomas was our damage control officer. He quickly put a yeoman in charge of central stations and took over as commanding officer on the conning tower.

In quick succession we were hit by two bombs and a torpedo. One of those bombs hit the anchor wrenches and broke the elevation screw. This decommissioned our turret.

This was followed by more bombs. Our casualties were lying all over the ship. It looked like our whole bow was on fire. A bunch of us were doing our best to hose down the area.

Then came the big explosion. The *Arizona* seemed to erupt like a volcano. Several of our sailors were actually blown into the water from the *Arizona*'s blast.

What happened next was truly astonishing. The *Nevada* actually got under way. We headed for the entrance to Pearl Harbor.

Apparently when Commander Mitsuo Fuchida, the working head of the Japanese striking force, realized what Commander Thomas was trying to do, he sent out the word to sink the *Nevada* as close to the entrance as possible. This would have been a disaster.

My God, it seemed every Japanese plane went after us. I don't know if Thomas received orders or if he acted on his own. But he saw immediately what they were up to. He turned the *Nevada* toward Ford Island. He was now trying to beach her. Thank God, he was successful. We ran aground on the beach at Ford. They now call the place where we beached "Nevada Point." From then on we were stationary, firing at every plane that came at us.

And they were still coming. One bomb went right through to the captain's cabin. It killed the captain's orderly and his mess attendant. All told I believe we had sixty-five men killed and at least that many wounded.

Our biggest problem after the second wave had passed was getting food. It was December 9 before I could get a halfway decent meal and a shower. We ended up sleeping in an auditorium ashore for several days.

There was a bit of black humor that I must not forget to mention. At 0800 each morning in port our band would play the "Star-Spangled Banner" as we held colors. The day of the attack was no exception. The National Anthem had just started when our band first noticed the Japanese planes. About halfway through the song everyone in the band realized what was happening.

So, nothing interferes with the "Star-Spangled Banner" and finish it they did. But they had to have broken all records for speed during the playing of that second half.

Well, I served throughout the war in the Navy. But every time I'd come back into Pearl, I looked at that narrow slip at the entrance. My God, if the Japanese had sunk the *Nevada* in the entrance, we couldn't have used Pearl for six months.

Jack Stoeber Changes His Mind

◆

I first thought I'd make a career out of the Navy. I got to Pearl Harbor on December 8, 1940, almost a year to the day before the Japanese attack.

To me, Pearl was great duty. My uncle worked in the Navy yard there. Our family was pretty close. I made my uncle's house my headquarters in Oahu. I saw a part of the island that most servicemen didn't see.

They had assigned me to the U.S.S. *Whitney*. On the morning of December 7 I was getting ready to go ashore when they sounded General Quarters. I had just gotten out of the shower. My battle station was on a .50 caliber machine gun and I ran to it. Then came a shock. There were the Japanese planes and we had no ammunition.

You see, we had been told to place all our ammo below decks.

So, there was only one thing to do. I ran below and picked up a box of .50 caliber bullets. To this day I don't know how I lifted it—hell, I only weighed about 140 pounds—but I got it topside.

By the time I got to my gun, my loader was also there. I strapped myself in and he loaded the gun. I started firing and didn't stop until the Japanese had left.

OK. I'm sure you've been told by lots of gunners that they shot down some planes. Please note that I'm not saying that I shot one down. I did pour several slugs into one plane, but it was in a glide anyway. He crashed over in a cane field. I'll bet you there were ten gunners who felt that kill was theirs.

There is one thing that did happen that I can remember clearly. I remember watching someone running up our battle flag. I can't describe the pride I felt as I saw Old Glory waving in the breeze. I just kept firing that machine gun.

Well, things all seem so different now. It appears to me that they don't even teach history the way they used to. They lump it in with some other courses and call it all Social Studies. It's just the old-timers like us who still love the flag.

Corporal James Brown,
1st Marine Defense Battalion,
Wake Island Detachment

◈

I was born and raised in the state of Colorado. When I was a youngster, my family took me to California for a vacation. The place in that state that really impressed me was the Marine Corps Recruit Depot in San Diego. That was for me. When you ask young boys what they want to be when they grow up, they'll answer, "firemen, ballplayers, movie stars, policemen," just to name a few.

Not me, I was going to be a Marine. No ifs or buts about it. That was it. So when I reached eighteen, I enlisted in the Corps and I stayed twenty-five years.

So, right off the bat, one of the things I liked the best about the Corps was its size. It was roughly seventeen thousand strong; that made it smaller than the New York City Police Department. As the years went by, it seemed that you knew most of the men in the Corps. It was just one big club.

There was one thing that wasn't much fun and that was advancement. Back in those days you could usually count on a stripe for each enlistment. If a man was a buck sergeant, he would usually have three hash marks. And he had to be on the ball to keep his advancement moving. Hell, we had PFCs with four hash marks all over the Corps.

Of course this all changed when war came. Most of the pre-war regulars quickly became sergeants or above because they were needed as leaders for the new outfits the Corps was putting together.

OK. Sometime in 1940, the Corps started to organize defense battalions. These were Marine antiaircraft units that were to be set up on the islands in the Pacific. Palmyra, Johnson, Wake, and Oahu were to each have one. The following year, I ended up in the 1st Marine Defense Battalion. Scuttlebutt had us going to Johnson Island and very soon.

Then our orders were changed. You know what they say. Don't anticipate commands unless you have them in your hands. Half of our battalion ended up going to Wake. I was in that half. But before we were to leave Oahu, they were to give us tetanus shots.

This was something new for the Navy. So, of course, it had to be fouled up. As they wanted us at Wake as soon as possible, they decided they'd give us double shots instead of two separate ones.

Hell, what a disaster! Half the group thought they were dying. My God were they sick, puking all over the place. But it only lasted a few days. Then we headed way out in the Pacific toward Wake.

In the meantime, my enlistment was up, but all discharges were frozen. There was no way they were going to start losing people with Hitler running wild all over Europe and the situation with Japan getting stickier all over the place.

Tojo became premier of Japan in October of '41. This put Japan firmly in the hands of the Army. Who knew what they were planning.

Anyway, in July and August our battalion started landing on Wake. And there was a catastrophe when we landed.

You see, our commanding officer was to be one Major Hahn. We didn't know much about him except that he would occasionally take a drink, or two or three and so forth.

Hell, when we were unloading his gear, one of his trunks fell overboard. It turned out to be the one that had his booze in it.

Scuttlebutt had it that there were tears in his eyes as he watched it going down.

Whatever, Hahn was soon relieved of command. I'll bet he was glad to go. His successor was Major James Patrick Sinot Devereux. J.P.S., as we first called him, was a stickler for the book.

This brings up a touchy subject. Devereux was in charge of the four hundred or so Marines on the island. However, when Naval Commander Winfield Scott Cunningham arrived in November, he took over the command of Wake. Devereux reported to Cunningham. But even today when you ask people who should know who was in command of Wake, they may well answer Devereux. So be it.

Well, my battalion officer was also the post exchange officer. So he decided to make me the beer steward.

"OK, Brown," he said, "I am putting you in charge of the beer, but don't drink it all."

What a deal. My buddies called me the Beer Baron. Today when we have a Wake Island Survivor reunion, someone will always give me the business. Remember, when I retired I was a captain. But a former Marine will come up to me and snicker.

"Captain James Brown. Baloney! I knew you when you pedaled beer in our slop chute at Wake."

I only had three types of beer. Millers, Budweiser, and something called Lucky Lager. Bud and Millers were by far the most popular. When I'd run out of Bud and Millers, I had to give everyone the Lager. Boy did they bitch!

"For chrissake, Baron, get rid of that panther piss."

So, sometimes I had to ration the Bud and Millers. When one of the men who didn't like beer would come up for his share, I'd give it to him even though I knew he was getting it for his buddies. So what.

Now, let me tell you a little about Wake. It was rather shaped like a V. In the middle was Wake Island. The left arm of the V was called Wilkes Island, while the right arm was named Peale

Island. There was a small water opening between Wake and the other two.

All three were quite small. They certainly didn't look like much. As a matter of fact, we didn't even realize the island was there until we were practically on top of it.

So, it didn't take long for us to realize that things were going to be different under Devereux than under Hahn. The new major had the reputation of being a martinet back in San Diego and it was well earned.

Take the time he read me off from asshole to appetite. It was about the same time that the Japanese diplomat (Saburo Kurusu) stopped off at Wake on his way from Tokyo to Washington. Our little island was a stopover for Pan Am planes going to and from Tokyo.

Well, our postal clerk was an old-time gunnery sergeant named Boozer. I think he was a WWI veteran. Old Boozer couldn't drive diddly squat. Believe it or not, fifty years ago, most Marines didn't have a license; I did. They got ahold of a side-car motorcycle and I would drive the old gunny over to the Pan Am Hotel and pick up our mail. I had driven over to the hotel one day when the major walked up behind me.

"Brown," he yelled, "what the hell are you dressed for, a beach party?"

I was stunned. I was well over six feet tall in those days and Devereux couldn't have been more than five feet seven inches. As I looked down on him, I realized that the way I was dressed was fine under Hahn. Obviously, it wasn't under Devereux. He continued his tirade.

"You are never, never to come near this hotel without a full-length khaki shirt and a field scarf. You are a Marine, not a beach-comber."

He wanted a tight ship at Wake. You know his name was J. P. S. Devereux. His nickname soon became "Just Plain Shit" Devereux.

But, I'll tell you, I got to know him real well at our reunions after the war. He knew at Wake we were a lot closer to some Japanese bases than we were to Pearl Harbor. He had to have us in tow if the Japanese attacked.

And when we were captured, it was the major who kept telling us we were Marines. I am sure we would have lost more Marines in captivity than we did if it weren't for Major Devereux. I salute his memory.

Now, remember we were only on Wake five months or so before December 7. During that time, things could be dull as hell, but nothing like what they would have been if we'd been there a year or two. After the war, I talked to Marines who were at Palmyra and Johnson. They told me they almost went nuts in those isolated spots.

We did have our social life if you want to call it that. A good deal of it revolved around the slop chute and the poker games.

So, I decided I'd make the boys feel at home. I let my sideburns grow long and I grew a real Wyatt Earp mustache. I looked like an old-time bartender. My buddies loved it, but I am not that sure about the officers.

The real entertainment, however, was the Jaw Bone Poker games. They called it that because half the players were always playing on credit. Payday came once a month, at which time the losers had to pay up.

Anyway, sometime around the first of December, we heard that a Japanese carrier had been spotted on our side of the neutralized area. This was a boundary line set up by the two countries. Capital ships were not to cross this line. After the war started, we all felt that carrier was part of the force that hit Pearl.

A day or two later, eight Grumman Wildcat airplanes arrived at Pearl under the command of Major Paul Putnam, USMC. They had come in a task force headed by the U.S.S. *Enterprise*. Bill Halsey had command of the operation. His orders were to shoot at any Japanese force that got in his way. They didn't call Halsey "Bull" for nothing. This made all of us realize we were sitting ducks if the war started.

Well, as you know, it did start on the morning of December 8, Wake time. I'd say the Japanese struck at Wake four or five hours after they bombed Honolulu.

Immediately after we got the word from Pearl, four of our twelve Wildcats were sent out on patrol. The major sounded battle stations for all troops. When we heard the bugler blow "To Arms," we all turned to.

All right, there is one thing I can remember vividly. Considering that we were really in trouble, our morale was especially high. There were only about four hundred of us. We knew we would be hit by a much larger force and that we were bound to be bombarded by air and by sea. Nevertheless, most of us were spoiling for some action. As our trucks were delivering us to our battle stations, we rode by the one thousand or so construction workers on the island. We were yelling to these men, "See you in Tokyo," things like that.

There was one thing we lacked and it was to cost us dearly. We had no radar. We had no idea when the Japanese were coming.

Eventually, we heard some planes roaring. At first, we felt they were ours. We hoped so anyway. Then we saw those flaming assholes on the wings.

My God, did they work us over! When they were through with their devilry, we took stock.

Wow! The island was devastated. Seven of our eight sitting planes were blown to bits along with most of the pilots. They had been killed trying to get their airships into the air. The Pan American Hotel was gutted. A good deal of our oil supply seemed to be burning and there were other fires burning all around.

And our workers weren't spared. Fifty of them were casualties. Their boss was a big Irishman named Teters. He had been an Army sergeant in France in 1918. He was a great help to us during the battle.

OK, we were hurt badly, but nowhere near as badly as the Japanese pilots told their admiral. Apparently they told their leaders that all they had to do was some mopping up. This wasn't to be the case. So, a few days later, the Japanese started to assault our island.

Now, do you remember that remark of the American officer at Bunker Hill, "Don't shoot until you see the whites of their eyes"?

Well, that's what Devereux had in mind. These two destroyers kept boring in on us and the major kept sending out the word.

"Don't shoot yet, don't shoot yet," was the word we were getting.

Hell, they were getting close enough for us to throw rocks at them. Finally, the major gave us the word.

"Blow 'em to hell," he said, and we let them have it. Three-inchers, five-inchers, and small fire, everything we had was thrown at them.

In the meantime, Major Putnam and Hank Elrod were bombing the Japanese cruisers. I know that Elrod shot down two of their planes. If I am not mistaken, the other pilots also shot down some. Before the surrender, either our pilots or our ground fire accounted for twenty-one Japanese planes. If we had had radar and could have put all twelve of our original planes in the air, God knows how much more damage we would have done.

But our pilots surely did a great job with what we had. Their squadron number was VMF-211. One of their pilots, Henry Elrod, received the Congressional Medal of Honor posthumously. When we were out of planes, our surviving pilots fought with the ground force. I believe Elrod was killed the last day of the battle.

However, I don't want to say that our air force was the most important part of the battle. It was our artillery, machine gun, and rifle fire that beat back that first assault. I believe it was the only time during the Pacific war that an amphibious landing was denied to an attacking force.

This caused astonishment back in Tokyo. To them, the Japanese military was invincible. They knew how many men we had. The order went out to the admiral in charge of the Japanese task force to take Wake at all cost. We knew from then on we could expect an air raid at least every twenty-four hours. And once they had all their ducks in a row, they'd overwhelm us.

During this period, we were constantly taking casualties. You know how important a gunnery sergeant is to a Marine unit. I sometimes used to think they ran the Corps. My battery's gunnery sergeant was one of those killed. His name was Jonathan Wright, and he was one hell of a Marine. His whole side was blown away. I also took some shrapnel from the same bomb that killed Wright.

The damage to our gear was also brutal. One of our guns was so badly damaged, we had to bore aim it.

Anyway, by the time the twenty-third of December arrived, the Japanese were beside themselves with anger. When I woke up early that morning, I knew their frustrations were soon to be over. As I looked out to sea, it appeared half the Japanese Navy had surrounded us. We wouldn't be able to stop them again. We all got ready to make them pay dearly for this little island in the sun, in the middle of nowhere, though.

So, early in the morning, they came. By this time, I was back at the command post with Devereux. It seemed to me that they deliberately beached a destroyer so their troops could jump right off onto the island. From then on it was one big firefight. As vicious as it was, I believe we were holding our own, especially on Wilkes Island, which was definitely in our hands.

Major Putnam had a small command in a particularly brutal hand-to-hand struggle with the Japanese. He was finally hit in the neck and passed out. Captain Elrod had grabbed a Thompson submachine gun and was doing his best to eliminate all the Japanese on the island. He was finally cut in half.

A young second lieutenant named Art Poindexter was in great shape. He had put together fifty or so Marines and felt he was a long way from finished.

But Commander Cunningham was the man on the spot. Remember, he not only had the Marines to worry about, but also the one thousand plus civilians. The Japanese were on Wake and would continue to grow in number. I didn't realize it at the time, but the Japanese admiral was catching all kinds of hell from Tokyo about their failure to take the island.

So, as I saw it, Cunningham had two choices. Surrender, even though we were still fighting, or, in a day or so, be annihilated. After all, we had certainly given the Japanese a message—"The U.S. Marines are no pushover." Cunningham decided to surrender. I recall that one PFC, Bob Stevens, was the last Marine killed on the island. He was with Captain Platt, one Marine unit that was still fighting. I think he was strafed.

Well, the Japanese took over. The way they looked at us, I felt they were going to kill us all. Then when they hog-tied us and sat us down, I was sure of it.

And today, as I look back, I still think that was the plan. But then their big-shot admiral came ashore. I think he realized that the whole world had admired the struggle we had put up. If they killed us all, there was no way it could be covered up.

But he couldn't stop one atrocity that the Japanese committed that I'll never forget. They took five of our men at random. I think it was three sailors and two of our sergeants. They then beheaded them. This not only angered us, but it puzzled us greatly. Above all, we wondered why those five and why did they do it at all?

Now here's what we were told. It was done because we had killed so many Japanese during the battle. Well, what the hell? It was a battle. People get killed in battle.

Well, they moved us to Japan. Here I got the word from an English-speaking Japanese.

"Whatever you do, if a guard is giving you hell, don't look him in the eye, look at the ground. If he feels you are defiant, he will clout you or worse."

I also found out not to say the word "monkey." That was a real no-no. It seems that before the days of recorded time, the Chinese felt that the sun gods lived in Japan. To appease them, they would drop off young virgins for the gods. The only living things in Japan at this time were the apes and monkeys. The Chinese felt that most of these young girls mated with the apes and the Japanese race was born. So, if one of the guards even heard you mention the word "monkey," you were in trouble.

Anyway, most of us did survive. Some of us even stayed in the Corps.

Now here's one for you. One of our pilots, Frank Tharin, not only survived, but he had three stars when he was killed in an automobile accident many years later.

Frank went to Korea as did I. But poor Frank. He was shot down and captured by the Chinese. After about four years as a guest of the Japanese, he ends up spending two more years as a prisoner of the Chinese.

Big Wright of Wake Island

◆

I spent three days visiting with forty or so veterans of the heroic U.S. Marine defense of Wake Island. Hopelessly outnumbered, 450 Marines held off thousands of Japanese troops for sixteen days.

The Marines' stand infuriated the Japanese. If there was one thing sacred to the Japanese besides their emperor, it was the Imperial Navy. Tokyo knew approximately how many Marines were on Wake. They expected the capture of the island to take no longer than a day or so. It didn't work out that way. What was left of the Marines were captured on December 23.

"When we got to China," one of the 1st Defense Battalion's veterans told me, "someone got ahold of an old English language newspaper. The Imperial Navy claimed in that paper that the Americans were armed with three 14-inch railroad guns."

"Oh, yes," claimed another veteran, "that was the *Shanghai Times*. I read it also. Hell, all we had were three- and five-inchers. And not too much ammunition for them."

"Yeah," said the first vet, "but we had enough to sink three destroyers and badly damage a cruiser on December 11."

What these men remembered was right. The full-scale Japanese attack on December 11 was supposed to quickly overrun the Marines. No, sir! On that one day alone the Marines undoubtedly inflicted as many casualties on the Japanese as there were Marine defenders.

These vets now enjoy discussing the battle when among other Marines. There is one thing they will always discuss and that's their platoon sergeant. Many Marines will tell you that sergeants run the Corps.

Well, there was a Victor MacLaughlin, John Wayne, and Clint Eastwood all rolled into one with the 1st Marine Corps Defense Battalion on Wake. His name was Jonathan Wright and his nickname was Big. This was because he weighed somewhere in the vicinity of 325 pounds. Legend has it that when Wright got to Wake Island they unloaded him in a cargo net.

"Big was something else," a vet told me. "You should have seen him eat. As a sergeant he'd always get special treatment in the mess hall."

"I'll say," reiterated another Wake Island Marine. "Big could eat eight eggs and ask for more. And beer," he continued, "they used to say Big could consume a keg of beer and still be on his feet."

Well, I don't know about that, but the Corps used to love its characters. If you were colorful and a great Marine, you became part of Marine Corps lore. Like Dan Daley, Lou Diamond, and Louie Cukela.

Anyway, Big Wright was quite close to being in their class.

Another Wake Island man joined the group.

"So, you're talking about Sergeant Big. Don't forget his lucky silver dollar he picked up down in Nicaragua when the Marines were chasing the Sandinistas. We were told that if Big got into a firefight, he'd hold that silver dollar in his hand and shout out to the Marines:

" 'Don't worry, boys. Nothing is going to happen to me. I've got my lucky dollar in my hand.'

"And I'll tell you something else. He could really run. He'd been in the Corps for four or five cruises. When he'd run, it sounded like a herd of horses. He would have made a great pro football player today.

"Of course, he was way overweight for the Corps, but he was so fast you didn't realize he carried so much extra baggage."

Well, whatever, one thing the sergeant did was die well. He was in charge of the three-inchers. There was a bunker where the three-inchers were located. The Marines were having air raids constantly. When the Japanese planes would come over, all the gunners would jump into the bunker. Everybody but Big Wright, that is. Big was just too big to get in. So, he'd mass his huge bulk at the entrance to the bunker.

Well, a bomb did come down and Wright absorbed most of it. Only one man was slightly injured inside the bunker but the mammoth sergeant was killed instantly.

There was a gruesome scene coming up. They buried what was left of the sergeant. Then a day or two later another bombing raid came over and exhumed Big Wright. One of the vets told me the mangled sergeant's huge corpse was not a pleasant sight to see.

But the gruesome sights had just started. It was a very heady group of the emperor's pilots who had blasted the Americans at Oahu. A few hours later they had expected another easy victory at Wake Island. They were in for a surprise.

I asked a Wake Island defender to tell me about the island.

"Oh, it was a shitty little place in the middle of nowhere," he said, "but we sure as hell didn't want to give it to the Japs."

If the Marines' defense of Wake Island did anything, it showed the Japanese they were in for a long, bloody war.

Alan Wolfley

◈

Al is from Rockford, Illinois, and has proudly told me that's the second largest city in Illinois. Join us, Al.

In the summer of '41, I had just graduated from high school. I had still not decided where I wanted to go to college. I liked the idea of Northwestern. One of my older brothers had gone there. My father said that my brother had majored in beer partying. So it was no dice for me as far as Dad was concerned. He had suggested a place called Cornell College out in the cornfields of Iowa. That wasn't for me. I felt Dad could come up with something a little better than that.

Anyway, that summer of '41 was sure exciting for our family. Dad had gone to France in 1918 with the 33rd Illinois National Guard. The 33rd had seen some hard action over there. My father had always felt America was snuckered into that war and he surely didn't want to see America going back into France with our guns blazing in '41.

Besides, FDR was an ardent interventionist. That meant Dad had to be an isolationist. He disliked Roosevelt with a vengeance. Frank Knox was an old friend of our family. When Frank joined Roosevelt's cabinet, my father felt betrayed, but he got over it.

Well, I still wasn't enrolled in any college and I was beginning to wonder what the hell was I going to do.

Then came the light. My father was having lunch with a judge friend of his. Dad gave the judge the whole story. He finished up with a question.

"Judge, where did you go to college?"

"Middlebury, '03," answered the judge, "a great school up in Vermont." Then the judge started selling my dad on Middlebury.

Well, that's how I ended up in Vermont a week or two before the semester started. By December I was really settled in. Loved the place.

Now, you wanted to know just what was I doing on December 7.

OK. Do you remember those crazy Rube Goldberg inventions fifty or so years ago? I was set up like one of those with four extension wires coming out of a major socket in the ceiling. I was leaning back in my chair, listening to Toscanini on the radio, and reading English history.

Jeez, when that announcer broke into Toscanini to report the Japanese attack, my chair went out from under me and I fell back on my ass, with the wires going every which way.

There I was, shocked out of my wits and livid with anger toward the Japanese.

That night a group of us went over to the Treadway Inn. Everyone was talking about the war even though we knew very little about the attack on our ships at Pearl.

However, slowly but surely the reports were coming in and they weren't very good. The Japanese certainly got the jump on us but we came back strong.

I finished out the year and then joined the Air Corps. I was shot down over Yugoslavia and made my way to the Adriatic with the help of some partisans. When the war ended, I was a major.

Conclusion

◆

How does one draw a conclusion to what happened at Pearl Harbor in 1941?

No matter what is said, while the Japanese ambassador to the United States was getting ready to go over to Secretary Hull's office and talk peace, Japanese airplanes were bombing an unsuspecting American military force on the island of Oahu.

To the aging Americans today, who were stationed at Oahu on December 7, 1941, the Japanese attack was nothing but murder. You can talk all you want about war being nasty anyway, but you are not going to change the minds of these veterans.

As far as I am concerned, Japan's attack was barbaric.

Yes, it can be said that Japan paid in full for starting a war with the United States. A nation has to be completely controlled by a military dictatorship to deliberately pick a fight with the most powerful nation in the world.

Of course, one can point to Japan's remarkable economic growth since the end of World War II as one of the truly miraculous industrial comebacks in the history of mankind. But would this incredible industrial and financial bonanza have occurred if Japan had not bombed Pearl Harbor? Yes or no, take your pick.

However, as the common denominator throughout *"This Is No Drill!"* is the Japanese attack on December 7, let's look at it purely from a military standpoint. If we do this, the Japanese military comes out as moronic. Did they really think the U.S. would not fight to the death after the Pearl Harbor attack?

The only chance Japan had to escape her doom would have been to turn back her task force once she heard there were no American carriers at Pearl. The fact was there were many Japanese admirals and American admirals also who felt the battleships were still king.

The stark truth is the Japanese Navy and her merchant fleet were utterly destroyed by America's land-based and carrier-based planes and also that underrated offensive weapon in the Pacific war, the American submarines.

Bibliography

In penning oral history I normally do not include a bibliography. However, for *"This Is No Drill!"* I did need to do a great deal of research. The following books were used by me at one time or another. The amazing thing is that much of the research material I used can be found in several of these books:

Albright, Harry. *The Japanese War Machine*. Secaucus: Chartwell Books, 1976.

——. *Pearl Harbor: Japan's Fatal Blunder*. New York: Hippocrene Books, 1988.

Berry, Henry. *Make the Kaiser Dance*. New York: Doubleday & Co., 1978.

——. *Semper Fi, Mac*. New York: Arbor House, 1982.

Costello, John. *The Pacific War*. Rawson Wade, 1981.

Creamer, Robert. *Baseball in '41*. New York: Viking Penguin, 1991.

DiMaggio, Dom with Bill Gilbert. *Real Grass—Real Heroes*. New York: Zebra Books, 1990.

Durant, John. *The Dodgers*. New York: Hastings House, 1948.

Goldstein, Richard. *Super Stars and Screwballs*. New York: E. P. Dutton & Co, 1991.

Gottesman, Ronald. *Focus on Citizen Kane*. New York: Prentice-Hall, 1976.

Halsey, III, William J. Bryan. *Admiral Halsey's Story*. New York: McGraw-Hill Book Co., 1947.

Harley, Foster. *Pacific Battle Lines*. The Macmillan Co., 1944.

Hoehling, A. A. *The Week Before Pearl Harbor*. New York: W. W. Norton & Co., 1963.

Huie, William. *The Revolt of Mamie Stover*. Amereon Ltd., 1954.

Ienaga, Saburo. *The Pacific War*. New York: Pantheon Books, 1978.

Iriye, Akira. *Power & Culture: The Japanese-American War 1941–1945*. Cambridge: Harvard University Press, 1981.

Ishimaru, Tota. *Japan Must Fight Britain*. Harrisburg: Telegraph Press, 1936.

Johnson, Staley. *Queen of the Flat-Tops*. New York: E. P. Dutton & Co., 1942.

Jones, James Earl. *From Here To Eternity*. New York: Scribner Publishing, 1951.

Ketchum, Richard M. *On Borrowed Time*. New York: Random House, 1989.

Kinkle, Rodger. *The Complete Encyclopedia of Popular Music and Jazz 1900–1950*. Arlington House, 1974.

Klungman, William. *1941*. New York: Harper & Row, 1971.

Layton, Edwin T. *And I Was There*. New York: William Morrow & Co., 1985.

Lord, Walter. *Day of Infamy*. New York: Henry Holt & Co., 1957.

Mersky, Peter B. *U.S. Marine Corps Aviation 1912 to the Present*. Baltimore: The Nautical & Aviation Publishing Company of America, 1983.

Morris, Samuel Eliot. *The Two Ocean War*. Boston: Little, Brown & Company, 1963.

Mosley, Leonard. *Hirohito*. Englewood Cliffs: Prentice-Hall, 1966.

Munder, Barbara and Joe Louis, Jr. *Joe Louis—50 Years An American Hero*. New York: McGraw-Hill Co., 1988.

Murphy, Edward. *Heroes of World War II*. Novato: Presidio, 1990.

The NFL Official Encyclopedia of Pro Football. New York: Macmillan, 1977.

Potter, John Dean. *Yamamoto*. New York: Viking, 1965.

Prange, Gordon W. with Donald M. Goldstein and Katherine Dillon. *At Dawn We Slept*. New York: McGraw-Hill, 1981.

———. *God's Samurai*. Bassey's (U.S.) Inc., 1990.

―――. *Pearl Harbor: Verdict of History*. New York: McGraw-Hill, 1985.

―――. *December 7, 1941*. New York: McGraw-Hill, 1988.

Schultz, Duane. *The Battle For Wake Island*. New York: St. Martin's Press, 1978.

Smith, S. E., ed. *The United States Navy in World War 2*. New York: William Morrow & Co., 1965.

Toland, John. *The Flying Tigers*. New York: Random House, 1970.

―――. *The Rising Sun* (2 volumes). New York: Random House, 1970.

Wiley, Mason. *Inside Oscar*. New York: Ballantine Books, 1986.